STORIES IN LOG AND STONE

STORIES IN LOG AND STONE

THE LEGACY OF THE NEW DEAL IN MINNESOTA STATE PARKS

DAVID R. BENSON

MINNESOTA DEPARTMENT OF NATURAL RESOURCES

Published by the Minnesota Department of Natural Resources
Written by David Benson
Production, editing, photo selection and captions by Joel Stedman, Minnesota State Parks
Book and cover design by Marian Lansky, Clarity, Duluth, Minnesota
Printed in the United States of America on recycled paper.

The publishers gratefully acknowledge the resources and assistance of the Minnesota Historical Society.

Thanks to our visitors who make purchases in Minnesota State Park Nature Stores. Proceeds from these sales goes towards resource management and interpretive projects.

Publisher's Cataloging-in-Publication Data

Benson, David R.
Stories in log and stone : the legacy of the New Deal in Minnesota state parks / by David R. Benson.
St. Paul, MN : Minnesota Dept. of Natural Resources, Division of Parks and Recreation, 2002.
p.   cm.

Includes bibliographical references.
ISBN 0-9657127-1-0
1. Parks—Minnesota—History. 2. Park facilities—Minnesota—History. 3. Civilian Conservation Corps (U.S.)
4. United States. Works Projects Administration. 5. United States. National Youth Administration.
6. Minnesota—History. 7. Minnesota—Description and travel. 8. New Deal, 1933-1939.
9. United States—History—1933-1945.
I. Minnesota. Dept. of Natural Resources. Division of Parks and Recreation. II. Title.
III. Legacy of the New Deal in Minnesota state parks

SB482.M6 B46 2002
363.68/09776—dc21   CIP

In honor and memory of those enrolled
in the Civilian Conservation Corps,
Veterans Conservation Corps, Works
Progress Administration, and National
Youth Administration, and of their
families, and of the people who oversaw
the camps and the work that was done.

ACKNOWLEDGMENTS

Practically all of the information for this book was gathered by Minnesota Department of Natural Resources, Division of Parks and Recreation, Interpretive Services staff. My job has been the smaller one of squeezing it between the covers of a book.

Minnesota DNR employees who have kept the heritage of the New Deal alive laid the foundation for this project. Among the many such people who could be named, one stands out for his efforts over the course of many years: Ben Thoma, long time naturalist at Itasca State Park. Much of the basis for this book was constructed by the hard work and interest of this man. But for his foresight, much of what is contained here might never have come to light.

Other contributors to this book, past and present, include Rolf Anderson, Peter Gregorson, Bromley Griffin, Harley Heegard, Frederick Johnson, Amy K. Rieger, Al Salvaag, Edward Schubert, Harry Sperling, LeRoy Tufts, and Ray Welle.

Joel Stedman and Retta James-Gasser made many improvements to the text.

I thank Dr. Thomas W. Shaffer and Pamela, Jonas, and Lars Benson for their indispensable assistance in completing this book.

—David R. Benson

I learned a great many things during the production of this book. Minnesota is blessed with a tremendous natural and cultural heritage not the least of which is our New Deal legacy. Although this book focuses on Minnesota State Parks, evidence of this legacy can be found in our national and state forests, throughout our communities and across the United States.

I'd like to thank those agencies and organizations who have helped keep this legacy intact: The National Association of CCC Alumni, The National Archives, The US Forest Service, The National Park Service, The Minnesota Historical Society, The Iron Range Research Center, and the Minnesota Department of Natural Resources.

In addition to the outstanding staff of Minnesota State Parks, Interpretive Services, I'd like to recognize the following individuals: Kate Brady, Char Feist, Doug George, Marian Lansky, Joe Niznik, Dave Radford, and Bonnie Wilson.

—Joel Stedman

ABOUT THIS BOOK

PART I

"Hard Times and Hard Work" is a story of the Great Depression, Franklin Delano Roosevelt, and the New Deal agencies that worked in Minnesota State Parks: the Civilian Conservation Corps (CCC), the Veterans Conservation Corps (VCC), the Works Progress Administration (WPA), and the National Youth Administration (NYA). This section provides an overview of the era and an idea of what life was like for those who built our parks.

PART II

"The Legacy of the Park Builders" serves as a guide and reference to help you get the most out of visits to parks that still have structures remaining from this era. This section is arranged geographically. Information for each park includes notes on the history of the park and highlights of the New Deal structures that are present.

CONTENTS

HARD TIMES AND HARD WORK

CCC boys planting pine.

PROLOGUE

The feel of cool, damp rock under the hand; the echo of shoes shuffling across a cement floor; the deep, shady light inside at midday; the residual smell of thousands of campfires in a stone fireplace–these impressions of stone and timber picnic shelters formed a vivid image in my mind when

Kitchen Shelter (Lady Slipper Lodge), Gooseberry Falls State Park

I was a child. That image had a lot to do with my growing idea of what nature was, what a park was, what Minnesota was.

Picnic shelters–and many other kinds of structures–built of stone or logs are found throughout Minnesota. Because many of them are located in state parks, these structures have been preserved and most are still open to the public. Eat a picnic lunch sheltered by cool limestone walls at Whitewater. Step back in time to attend an interpretive program in Forest Inn at Itasca. Go swimming at the beach at Lake Shetek. Sway on the

Swinging Bridge at Jay Cooke. These parks and more than twenty others contain hundreds of historic structures.

Almost all of the stone and log buildings that exist in today's parks were built during the 1930s, during the Great Depression. The buildings we still use were envisioned, planned, and constructed by people organized under a group of government agencies that were created to "make work" for the poor. These agencies sprang from the desperation the country felt in the early 1930s. They were initiated by the new administration of President Franklin Delano Roosevelt to serve several purposes: to provide income for young, unemployed men to support their families; to inject money into the stagnant economy; to stave off the growing forces calling for revolution in the United States; and to take on tasks that couldn't have been accomplished in any other way.

These immense accomplishments included large parts of the infrastructure still in use today:

Lady Slipper Lodge, Gooseberry Falls State Park

highways, bridges, dams, airports, public buildings, erosion control projects, golf courses, parks, plazas, and sculptures. Millions of acres of trees were planted, speeding reforestation on the heels of the logging era that felled much of the nation's forests. The New Deal agencies also produced plays, books, school curricula, histories, and newspapers.

For many, however, the most enduring symbols of the New Deal are the stone and log buildings found in state and national parks across the United States. Under any other conditions, the labor involved in building these structures would have been prohibitively expensive.

The story of the New Deal and the legacy it left in our parks begins in the depths of the Great Depression, and it includes the sounds of song and laughter, the changing light of the seasons, and the smell of fires in barrel stoves, keeping young men warm through cold winters and hard times.

Inside barracks at Gooseberry Falls State Park

ONE
THE GREAT DEPRESSION AND THE NEW DEAL

Soup kitchens filled with hopeless souls ... bitter demonstrations in the streets ... wandering hobos ... families burdened with belongings traveling the highway–these are the images that filled the newspapers in March, 1933. The country was already in the depths of the Great Depression.

The Great Depression resulted from the near collapse of the nation's economy. Farmers had been sliding into hard times since shortly after World War I. By 1929, many were losing their farms. But much of the rest of the nation was oblivious to the impending catastrophe. The Roaring Twenties were good times in parts of the country.

Then, in October, 1929, the stock market crashed, and it became clear to everyone–hard times were at hand.

Once the stock market crashed, the rest of the economy fell like a house of cards. Large banks failed. Other banks were weakened as customers withdrew all their money. The disaster in rural areas spread to the cities, where people started to lose their homes. Citizens who had held respectable jobs were forced to go door-to-door, begging for food, clothing, or money. By late 1932, one-quarter of the work force (over 12 million people) was out of work.

In Minnesota, unemployment was 29 percent overall and 70 percent on the Iron Range. Property foreclosures were common. By 1933, one-seventh of all land in Minnesota was tax delinquent.

American City

On the Brink of Revolution

A sense of strangling desperation settled over the nation. Angry World War I veterans formed a Bonus Expeditionary Force (BEF), an "army" of protesters who marched to Washington, D.C. to demand early payment of their wartime service pensions. They built a shantytown, called Hoovertown, where they stayed while they pressed their demands. President Hoover responded by ordering the armed forces under the command of General Douglas MacArthur to remove the protesters, which they did with the use of guns, bayonets, and tear gas.

The veterans' army was not the only threatening presence of that day. Agitators such as Huey Long, a populist senator from Louisiana and Father Charles Coughlin, a radio personality, typified the widespread prevalence of radical ideas on both left and right. Communist groups such as the John Reed Clubs and the Young Communist League increased their memberships. Americans were desperate for change.

FDR and the New Deal

Franklin Delano Roosevelt (FDR) was inaugurated the 32nd president of the United States in 1933. In one of his campaign speeches, FDR had said, "The country needs and, unless I mistake its temper, the country demands bold, persistent experimentation. It is common sense to take a method and try it: If it fails, admit it frankly and try another. But above all, try something. The millions who are in want will not stand by silently forever while the things to satisfy their needs are within easy reach."

Candidate Roosevelt called for the employment of "a million men" to fight "a future of soil erosion and timber famine." This was his first mention of the

Minnesota farm family

Hard times at hand

Franklin Delano Roosevelt, 1933

general idea of the Civilian Conservation Corps. The concept was ridiculed by the Hoover Administration and other critics, and little else happened with the idea until after the election in November of 1932, when the Forest Service was asked to begin developing plans for putting 25,000 men to work in national forests.

FDR was inaugurated on March 9th. He immediately declared a "bank holiday," which closed all banks and allowed the monetary situation to stabilize. On March 21, Roosevelt asked Congress for immediate action on legislation to provide employment relief. This would enable him "to create a civilian conservation corps to be used in simple work, not interfering with normal employment, and confining itself to forestry, the prevention of soil erosion, flood control and similar projects." He estimated that 250,000 men could begin work by early summer. This mobilization would be larger than the one undertaken for World War I.

The idea was opposed by organized labor. They claimed that the proposed pay of $30 a month was too low and would undermine pay scales in the regular workplace. This argument was countered with the fact that if clothing, room, and board were figured in, the wages were much higher.

FRANKLIN DELANO ROOSEVELT
President of the United States, 1933-1945

Franklin Delano Roosevelt (FDR) was born in 1882 to a wealthy, New York family. He became a lawyer, a state senator, and Assistant Secretary of the Navy. He was stricken with polio, which left him with paralyzed legs in 1921, yet went on to serve as Governor of New York from 1928-1932.

When he defeated President Herbert Hoover in 1932, the Great Depression was sliding into its worst years. Though others had ideas about a national employment force, it was Roosevelt who made the CCC and the other New Deal work agencies a reality.

FDR, called "King Franklin" by some of his opponents, was the only U.S. president to be re-elected three times. He was president through most of the Great Depression, as well as World War II. He died in 1945, three weeks before the Germans surrendered.

FDR and friend, 1933

Furthermore, due to the age and need requirements, fewer than two percent of the 12 million unemployed at that time could enter the corps.

Others opposed the legislation as a misguided attempt to solve social problems by putting the unemployed young into an army, as Mussolini and Hitler had done in Italy and Germany. In response, Roosevelt emphasized that this corps was civilian; the Army was only involved because there was no other agency that could mobilize such a project. He told a press conference on March 22 that talk of militarization was "utter rubbish."

FDR was persuasive. He used radio to speak directly to people in their homes in masterful, short speeches he called "Fireside Chats." He held rollicking, informal press conferences that helped him gain support in the newspapers of the day. His efforts paid off in the passing of an unprecedented quantity of legislation in the first hundred days of his administration.

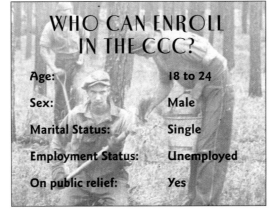

WHO CAN ENROLL IN THE CCC?

Age:	18 to 24
Sex:	Male
Marital Status:	Single
Employment Status:	Unemployed
On public relief:	Yes

The Emergency Conservation Work (ECW) bill cleared both houses on March 31. On April 5, the executive order was signed establishing the Civilian Conservation Corps (CCC) and making Robert Fechner its leader. Fechner was chosen for this position, officially titled Director of Emergency Conservation Work, partly because of his connection to organized labor.

The Civilian Conservation Corps was Roosevelt's "baby." At the beginning, he gave it his personal attention, and he required that all the details of setting it up be cleared through the White House. This created a paperwork jam, and by mid-May Roosevelt had to give up the details or risk damaging the program. He delegated the authority for recruiting to the Labor Department, camp organizing to the War Department, work projects to the Departments of Agriculture and the Interior; and he allowed Fechner to take a freer hand in running the program. On April 7, 1933, the first man was enrolled. Ten days later the first work camp opened: Camp Roosevelt in Luray, Virginia.

Even with just a few camps up and running, the CCC was helping FDR politically. On May 9, a new Bonus Expeditionary Force began arriving in Washington. Within two weeks, 3,000 poor, embittered veterans had arrived.

This time, instead of being driven out by the army, the men were housed at Fort Hunt, an army camp across the Potomac. They were fed three meals a day and were provided with medical service. They were serenaded by the Navy Band, and their leaders were invited to the White House. One day, Eleanor Roosevelt visited the fort, talking with the men individually and giving a speech about her reminiscences of the war. "Hoover sent the army; Roosevelt sent his wife," was what one vet said, and his comment typified how differently these men viewed the two presidents.

Throughout their encampment, the men were encouraged to disperse, though it is doubtful they would have done so without the promise of the CCC. The qualifications regarding age were waived, and over 2600 men accepted the offer of joining a CCC camp. This was the genesis of the Veterans Conservation Corps (VCC) camps that were among the first to open that summer.

"...THE ONLY THING WE HAVE TO FEAR IS FEAR ITSELF, NAMELESS UNREASONING, UNJUSTIFIED TERROR..."

—from FDR's Inaugural Address

ROBERT FECHNER
Director of the CCC from 1933-1939

Robert Fechner once said he was "a potato bug amongst dragonflies." His simple lifestyle was a contrast to the wealthy New Dealers around him. In 1933 he was still wearing the high-topped, hook-fastened shoes that had been popular at the turn of the century. When in Washington, he always stayed in the same, modest hotel room.

Fechner was born in Chattanooga, Tennessee in 1876. He apprenticed to a machinist in Augusta, Georgia and then worked as an itinerant machinist in Latin America until he returned to Savannah, Georgia in the late 1890s. He led a successful strike for a nine-hour day in 1901. By 1914, he had become a vice-president in the National Machinists' Union. He lectured on labor relations at Harvard and other universities.

During World War I, he helped negotiate settlements to railroad strikes. It was during this time that he met the Assistant Secretary of the Navy, Franklin Roosevelt. When organized labor opposed the CCC, Roosevelt reasoned that it would be best to hire a labor leader to run the agency, and Fechner got the job. He was hard working and honest, and he became the beloved "Big Boss" of CCC enrollees throughout the United States.

He crossed the country visiting camps, and he came to Minnesota on at least two occasions. He died unexpectedly in 1939. Near campsite #115 in what is today the Pine Ridge Campground at Itasca State Park, a low stone bears a metal plaque inscribed with the words, "In Memoriam, Robert C. Fechner, 1876-1939, First Director of the CCC from 1933-1939. Mr. Fechner Visited This Camp, June 6, 1939. Tablet Placed by Members of CCC Company 1785, World War Veterans."

FDR with Robert Fechner on his right at CCC camp, August 12, 1933

The CCC and the Launching of the New Deal

Just three days before Roosevelt took office, the movie, *Gabriel Over the White House*, was released. The movie portrays a president as a corrupt politician with no interest in the well being of the people. After a car crash nearly kills him, he is transformed into a man of compassion who launches a program of aggressive government activity. He feeds the unemployed, creates an "army of construction," and provides aid to farmers.

The movie shows that the idea of work camps was not new. Both California and Washington had worked with the Forest Service in running camps for the unemployed, and by 1932, several countries, including the Netherlands, Norway, Sweden, Denmark, and Austria had conservation camps.

Another source for FDR's idea for conservation camps came from his own love of the woods and the outdoors. He

CCC boys

had reforested much of his home in New York, and when he was governor, he sponsored several conservation initiatives. By the time he became president, the need for work on the land was pressing. Forests had once covered 800 million acres in the continental United States. By 1933, only 100 million acres remained. In this vast, logged-over area, erosion and forest fires were rampant. Roosevelt felt that much of this land could be used for recreation and resource renewal.

The CCC was the triumph of the New Deal. It was the first and perhaps the most popular of the dozens of large programs that came into existence in the 1930s. Roosevelt drew attention to it whenever he could. In a speech at Glacier National Park in 1934, he said, "This is just another example of our efforts to build not for today alone, but for tomorrow as well.…We are definitely in an era

Getting to work at Jay Cooke State Park

of building, the best kind of building–the building of great public projects for the benefit of the public and with the definite objective of building human happiness."

When FDR visited CCC camps in the state of Virginia in August, 1933, he liked what he saw. Chatting with "the boys" and reporters he said, "I wish I could spend a couple of months here myself. The only difference between us is that I am told you men have put on an average of twelve pounds each. I am trying to lose twelve pounds…More important, I have seen the boys themselves, and all you have to do is to look at the boys themselves to see that the camps themselves are a success."

The Continuing New Deal

The CCC was just one of dozens of pieces of legislation, programs, grants, and agencies that FDR proposed at the outset of his administration. Though he had campaigned as a fiscal conservative, he justified the change in light of the worsening depression. In his inaugural address, he had promised a "new deal" for the American people, and this is what his plan, and even his era, came to be called–The New Deal.

The second year of the CCC opened with 300,000 men enrolled, including 28,000 war veterans and 22,000 local experienced men. In the summer of 1934, the president increased

Some of the boys from Company 2710, Gooseberry Falls State Park

the strength of the CCC to 350,000 by additional enrollment in drought areas of the central states. Most of these were in the southern Great Plains. Among the few drought camps in Minnesota were Camden, Fort Ridgely, and Cottonwood River (Flandrau) state parks.

By April, 1935 the enrollment authorization was increased to 600,000, but by this time, economic conditions had improved somewhat, and a new requirement had been attached to the CCC: all enrollees had to come from the public relief rolls or be veterans. It was becoming difficult to find enough enrollees, and the goal was reduced to 500,000.

The Works Progress Administration

With a couple of years of New Deal success under his belt, FDR told the new Congress of 1935 that he wanted the government to find work for all able-bodied, destitute workers: "We must preserve not only the bodies of the unemployed from destruction but also their self-respect, their self-reliance and courage and determination." With that he proposed a single, new, much larger plan to supersede the legislation that launched the New Deal in 1933.

The largest and most controversial part of this plan was the Works Progress Administration or WPA. (In another reorganization in 1939, the name was changed to Works Projects Administration.) The CCC continued, but the WPA was to expand the provision of work far beyond the concept of the

THE MINNESOTA WPA STRIKE

Just as Minnesotans were beginning the Fourth of July holiday in 1939, Congress decided to reduce the hourly wage and extend the workweek of the WPA. When workers returned after a steamy holiday weekend, they learned of the changes. Many of them would receive half of what they had been getting. Though strikes were illegal, 18,000 WPA workers walked off the job in Minnesota alone. Sidewalks remained uncompleted, and roads sat unfinished. The WPA announced that any worker who didn't return to the job would be fired. Non-striking workers were given police escorts across picket lines. Each day brought more conflicts. On July 10, police used tear gas on strikers at a project in Minneapolis, and in the ensuing violence one worker was killed and 17 were injured. After the incident, Minneapolis withdrew police protection for workers, and the government was forced to negotiate. A settlement was reached on July 21. Though strikes had taken place in several cities, the federal government chose to prosecute workers in Minneapolis, possibly because of suspected Communist activity in the state. During the trial, it was revealed that 25 FBI agents had infiltrated the ranks of strikers. Eventually, 15 of the strikers served jail time.

WPA work project, Itasca State Park

CCC to include women and to remove the age limit. Anyone over the age of 18 was eligible to apply, depending upon need and employability. During the rest of the New Deal, the WPA provided about three-quarters of all relief employment, compared with one-eighth provided by the CCC, and one-eighth by all other agencies combined.

The primary legislation that created the WPA passed, but FDR had to battle to keep it from being changed by any amendments. Roosevelt threatened to veto the whole plan if it was changed, and he used his radio Fireside Chats to rally the people.

The WPA went well beyond the conservation

WPA map of projects in Minnesota

work undertaken by the CCC. WPA workers served hot lunches, recycled toys, operated recreation centers, taught literacy classes, staged plays, collected oral histories, wrote curricula, balanced accounting ledgers, and undertook many other jobs. In Minnesota, WPA writers wrote travel guides to the state and to the Arrowhead Region.

The work also included CCC-style conservation projects, including buildings, roads, and other structures in 19 Minnesota state parks. Because of the breadth of the WPA, enrollees probably worked in some of the parks in ways that are now lost to history. Since the CCC was gradually reduced in size through the late 1930s, WPA camps often finished projects begun by the CCC.

The WPA was a flexible program. Administrators were given guidelines about the program, but specifics were not mandated. Recruiters were free to seek experienced and qualified workers, and this was reflected in the high quality of the WPA structures in the state parks. During the first month of the program, 54,000 Minnesotans were hired. The program never employed more than three percent of Minnesota's population, but by the end, it was estimated that half a million people in the state had been enrolled in the WPA.

The WPA never gained the same political popularity that the CCC had enjoyed in its first years. The "white-collar work," provided by the WPA was criticized, but advocates of the program countered by pointing out that the children of these workers needed clothing and food as much as the children of blue-collar workers.

The WPA began on July 1, 1935 and was closed down June 30, 1943.

During these eight years, over 8 million individuals worked for the WPA. The average wage for all types of work over the course of the program was $54 a month.

During the 1930s, two and one-half percent of national work relief funds were channeled to projects within the arts. These children's posters appeared in a WPA exhibit in Virginia, Minnesota.

Minnesota Historical Society

The National Youth Administration

The National Youth Administration (NYA) was established as a sub-division of the Works Progress Administration on June 26, 1935. It provided work training for unemployed young people of both sexes (ages 17-22) and part-time employment for needy students. When adults became unemployed, many of them ended up taking part-time jobs that, in better times, would have been done by teenagers or young adults. This made the unemployment problem in this age group much worse, and the NYA was created to address this problem.

The NYA was responsible for building two rustic-style buildings at Lake Bemidji State Park. These are the only state park structures built by the NYA in Minnesota, and this may have been the largest NYA building project in the country. However, given the widespread presence of the program, it is likely that NYA enrollees played small roles at other state parks too. For example, since men from the camps at Itasca State Park advised the NYA during the construction of the buildings at Lake Bemidji, NYA youths may have also made their way to Itasca.

STORIES IN LOG AND STONE **21**

MNDNR

Picnic shelter built by the National Youth Administration, Lake Bemidji State Park

Most of the work of the NYA, however, was less enduring than log and stone buildings. The NYA did run some camps and educational centers, but, for the most part, it was a decentralized program. In many places, one youth would be assigned to a park, a school, or a county agency. They would help in whatever way they were asked. At Lake Bemidji, they also cleared vegetation from public areas and eradicated poison ivy.

Over 2.6 million young people had NYA jobs during its time. As World War II approached, the emphasis of the agency was shifted toward training for a possible war effort. The NYA was abolished at the end of 1943.

The Progress of the New Deal

In 1936, the CCC had achieved almost universal political acclaim. By this time, millions of Americans were surviving mainly on their wages from government work programs. Though the New Deal had opponents from the beginning, over the course of the decade there were no serious challenges to the basic idea of providing work for the unemployed. The federal work programs were well-established and on their way to building the parks of today.

National Park Service staff mapping and designing Fort Ridgely State Park

TWO

GETTING ORGANIZED: MINNESOTA AND THE NEW DEAL

From its controversial beginnings, the New Deal swept across the country like a dust storm. The daunting task of launching all of these programs required that existing agencies take on, sometimes reluctantly, the task of getting them started. The Labor Department was charged with recruiting, the War Department with inducting the enrollees, and the Departments of Agriculture and the Interior were in charge of overseeing the work projects.

Dust storm descends on downtown Minneapolis, 1938

George E. Luxton, courtesy of Minnesota Historical Society

The National Park Service

One agency of the Department of the Interior, the National Park Service (NPS), was eagerly waiting for the New Deal. Since the establishment of Yellowstone National Park in 1872, the park system had grown slowly and with little development. Over the course of the 1920s, however, the NPS had been preparing plans, in case an opportunity came along to carry them out on a large scale. When the CCC began, the NPS was ready with projects and plans that were ideal for the CCC: they furthered conservation aims, they didn't compete with private industry, and they were ready for implementation.

The scope of the New Deal work programs was, however, much larger than anyone had imagined just a few years earlier. The NPS went well beyond its initial agenda and began encouraging states to open parks in areas that were worthy of preservation but which probably

CCC boys hanging out at entrance to Jay Cooke State Park

NEW DEAL ALPHABET SOUP

AAA Agricultural Adjustment Act: a program to aid farmers

CCC Civilian Conservation Corps: camps for young men who worked on conservation projects

ECW Emergency Conservation Work: the original, legislative title of the CCC; changed officially to CCC in 1937

FDR Franklin Delano Roosevelt: president of the United States throughout the New Deal Era

FERA Federal Emergency Relief Administration: the original agency charged with dispensing money in the New Deal

LEM Local experienced man: an employee of the CCC

NRA National Recovery Administration: a program that aided struggling industries

NYA National Youth Administration: a work program for 17 to 22 year-olds

VCC Veterans Conservation Corps: camps for World War I veterans, who worked on conservation projects; part of the CCC

WPA Works Progress Administration (eventually renamed the Works Projects Administration)

MNDNR

wouldn't qualify for national park status.

Seven states opened their first state parks during the period. In all, 37 states started 350 new state parks. Minnesota, of course, had established its first state park in 1891, but the number of units in the state's system doubled during the New Deal.

Minnesota's Leaders

In Minnesota, all of the early work was delegated to the State Forestry Service, led by Grover M. Conzet. In 1935, the Division of State Parks was created by the legislature, and its first director, Harold Lathrop, took office. General design plans had to be approved by the National Park Service, but Lathrop approved all subsequent individual plans.

Lathrop, his assistant, Reuben Law, architect Ed Barber, and U.W. "Judge" Hella, who held several different positions during this period, all played pivotal roles in the development of the parks during the New Deal.

Early Enrollees

In Minnesota, enrollees first went to induction centers such as Fort Snelling for medical examinations. If they failed, they were given money to get back home. Many lied about their age, but officials often looked the other way. If they were accepted, they were organized into companies, equipped, and sent to work camps. (Later in the New Deal, much of this processing was taken care of right at the camps.) The War Department also was responsible for building and maintaining the camps, as well as housing, feeding, and clothing the employees.

JUDGE HELLA

Udert W. Hella, known as "Judge" since his youth, worked on several key projects in the 1930s and went on to have a great influence on the development of the state park system. Hella worked as a draftsman until the National Park Service hired him to be an engineering foreman at Scenic State Park in 1933. He transferred to Sibley State Park where he was Camp Superintendent. He went on to supervise the *Minnesota Park, Parkway, and Recreational Area Study*, which laid the groundwork for park development for decades. From 1937 to 1941, he supervised the Northern District of Parks, and during that time, he oversaw many of the projects that were completed in the Northeastern quarter of the state. He was named director of the entire parks division in 1953, and during his twenty years in that position, the state park system realized many of the goals that were set in the 1930s. Years after the New Deal, some of his co-workers still called him "the Inspector," based on one of his roles in the 1930s. Considering his work during the New Deal Era and his tenure as director, it would be hard to name another individual who had more influence on Minnesota State Parks as we know them today.

U.W. "Judge" Hella, Director, Minnesota State Parks, 1953 to 1974

CCC members leaving Fort Snelling for the Superior National Forest

"Along with a dozen others from Red Wing, I was transported to Fort Snelling for a week of induction and processing. At that time, a good-sized garrison of the regular army was stationed at the post. Many were grizzled veterans of long service who did not hesitate to voice their displeasure with a system that paid soldiers $21.00 per month as compared with the $30.00 that we were to receive."

–Frederick Johnson, Whitewater State Park

Some enrollees felt a little like cattle on the way to market. Harry Sperling, who worked at Itasca, lived only 25 miles from the park, but he was loaded up with 60 other recruits, whose train took them on a 100 mile journey through several neighboring communities en route to the park. Sperling said, "If we had known where we were going, we would have started out walking!"

Once they arrived at camp, they received uniforms and vaccinations: "The first thing that happened when we got to camp was they took us to the infirmary, or the first aid station, and we got our shots. I think it was typhus, typhoid, tetanus, and we got a scrape for tuberculosis. From there we went to the supply room. We drew our bedding, clothing, personal care kit, and I remember the shoes very well. They were all one size, large!" *–Edward Schubert, Itasca State Park*

For the first few months, all of the uniforms were military surplus. Later in the 1930s, recruits were issued regular uniforms, which they sometimes customized: "The sort of 'in'

Fresh recruits at St. Croix State Park

"Being the oldest one in the family among the children, I felt it my obligation to help support the family, and I entered into the CCCs."
—Raymond Noyes, Gooseberry Falls

Enrollees arrive at New London, bound for Sibley State Park

thing at the time was to take your pants and add a triangle piece of clothing to make them bell-bottoms when you first got to camp. The thing of it was that a lot of us cut the material out of our blankets. So when we came into camp, we checked our blankets. About half the fellows had part of their blankets cut off."
—*Edward Schubert, Itasca State Park*

Missing Home

For many Minnesota "boys," this was their first trip away from home. Homesickness was common in the CCC camps, so common that it was addressed in the enrollee's handbook: "Sometimes, after we get accustomed to living with one group we find it difficult or unpleasant to adjust ourselves to another group or another way of living. It is not

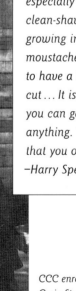

"They expected you to be clean, especially around your face, clean-shaven unless you were growing into a beard or a moustache. They expected you to have a haircut, a recent haircut ... It isn't like today, when you can get away with most anything. There were some rules that you observed."
—Harry Sperling, Itasca State Park

CCC enrollees at St. Croix State Park

> *"It was a seemingly desolate spot, but with the enthusiasm of all the boys, failure seemed to be out of the question."*
>
> *—an enrollee*

Camp SP-1, Itasca State Park, Summer, 1934

Getting acquainted at Itasca State Park

unnatural for us to feel so when we first leave home and start out in the world to live with other people. Some of us feel it more than others. Some of us think we just can't stand it . . . For a while they feel downright lonely. They can't get their home or the folks off their minds.

The best cure for homesickness is getting acquainted with a person who stands next to you, eats next to you or works next to you. If you feel an attack of homesickness coming on don't go off and mope for yourself, go out and play baseball or something else that will put you in personal contact with other enrollees. The first thing you know, a new form of life will creep in around you, and you will feel as much a part of things as you do when you are at home."

The camps–CCC, VCC, WPA, and NYA–would become home to thousands of enrollees over the course of the decade. These self-contained villages were the cradle and crucible of memories that stayed with the enrollees for the rest of their lives.

THREE

AT HOME IN THE WOODS: SETTING UP CAMP

Military Nature of the Camps

The agencies that set up the CCC camps ended up dividing control of the camps by using the clock. Once the workday was over, the camp and its inhabitants were overseen by the War Department. During the day, however, things were run by the agency conducting the work.

The War Department built the camps following the model of military barracks, and throughout the period, there was tension over just how "military" these camps were to be. The Army, which had only reluctantly taken on the work it was given, felt that it should have been given more control to go along with its burden. The army officers who were called to run many of the camps struggled to deal with these civilian/military camps. They often over-enforced regulations. In one year, CCC Director Fechner reinstated about half of the enrollees dropped by the Army for breaches of regulations.

Most of the camps set up by the agencies followed the original military plan. There would be rows of barracks, a mess hall, a kitchen, tool houses, and an infirmary. The camps, often located in remote areas, had to function as self-contained villages. Food, medical care, recreation, rest, and warmth had to be provided, along with the extensive infrastructure required to carry out the work. CCC camps were designed to house about 200 men, but WPA and NYA camps were often much smaller.

Army officers at VCC Camp, Ft. Ridgely State Park

Headwaters Camp at Itasca State Park illustrating typical camp layout

MNDNR

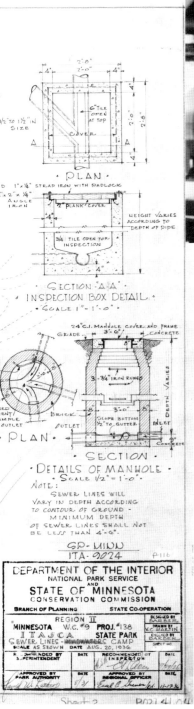

MNDNR

Inside the barracks, Ft. Ridgely State Park

> *"The barracks were very clean. I remember that. The floors were just spotless. They were wood floors. They were shiny white, I would say."*
> —Edward Schubert, Itasca State Park

The Men

To enroll in the CCC, a young man had to be an unemployed citizen between 18 and 24. Initially, recruits had to come from the welfare rolls, but this requirement was eventually dropped as the programs grew. Enrollees had to agree to serve for six months, to a maximum of two years. Veterans of any age were selected through a separate process. It was later, when the WPA was established, that women joined the work programs.

Enrollees received uniforms, housing, food, medical care, and $30 a month. They had to send $25 a month home to their families. Some families returned the money to the son who had earned it. Others needed the money to survive. The $5 that stayed in camp covered expenditures such as tobacco, candy, toiletries, and postage. Most recruits used up their $5 each month.

> *"It saved my family. I had a mother and three sisters that had to be fed. And there was not work for a teenager. But the CCC was a way out. My mother could support herself and my sisters on the $25 I sent home every month. Hard to believe, but that's the way it was in those days. A dollar was a dollar!"*
> —Warren Hill, Itasca State Park

Some men were selected as leaders and assistant leaders. The number of such "rated" men was limited to sixteen percent of the size of the company. Leaders received $45 a month; assistant leaders, $36 a month.

The men gained an average of eight to fourteen pounds in weight and about a half inch in height as a result of good food, regular schedule, and hard, physical work. The disease and mortality rates were below the national average for this age group.

Local Experienced Men–the LEMs

Since hundreds of thousands of young men were being turned loose, most with little prior experience, it was decided to hire about a dozen "Local Experienced Men" (LEMs) to advise each camp. Originally these men had to be recruited by the Labor Department, but after the first couple of years, this job was turned over to the states, who had a better handle on where such men were to be found.

> "They knew the country and how to survive and were in charge of the working parties. They knew how to handle dynamite, fell trees, use axes and crosscut saws. Without them we would have been lost."
>
> –an enrollee

DEPRESSION PRICES, 1932-1935

Bacon	22¢/pound
Bread	5¢/20 ounces
Butter	19¢/pound
Chicken	22¢/pound
Coffee	26¢/pound
Corn Flakes	1¢/ounce
Eggs	25¢/dozen
Flour	99¢/24.5 pounds
Ham	31¢/pound
Pork and beans	$1.00/20 large cans
Pork chops	20¢/pound
Potatoes	$1.35/100 pounds
Round steak	26¢/pound
Sour cream	9¢/pound

Cyril O'Bryen, local experienced man, second from left (sitting) with his crew from Gooseberry Falls State Park.

Ft. Ridgely VCC lays down the first course of stone for the park custodian's residence

The LEMs were older and they usually were hired because of their knowledge of woodcraft, masonry or welding. They often served as father figures in addition to their roles as leaders of the work.

Camp Populations

The majority of the men enrolled in New Deal work camps like the CCC were at the young end of the eligible age range 18, 19, or 20 years old. As men got older, they were more likely to be married and have families, and less likely to move off to a camp.

There was another large group of enrollees, however, between the ages of 40 and 44. These were the men of the VCC, born around the turn of the century, veterans during World War I (1914-1918). Though the VCC was always a small part of the CCC (around ten percent), many of these men were bachelors who stayed in the Corps for more than the usual six months to a year.

Minority Camps

American Indians were not originally eligible for the CCC, ostensibly because they already lived in "healthful outdoor surroundings." The Depression, however, drove many urban Indians back to the reservations, where the drought years repeatedly destroyed crops that supported the hard-pressed people. On April 14, 1933, the Emergency Conservation Work Act was extended to 14,400 American Indians.

American Indians in Minnesota worked in both the CCC and the WPA, and though none of their projects were within future state parks, their work, and the income it generated, helped get them through the Great Depression.

African-Americans were eligible for the CCC from the beginning, and eventually 200,000 African-Americans worked in the CCC, and many more in the WPA. Camps were, for the most part, segregated. Only two Minnesota state parks had African-American camps in their history: Temperance River and Fort Snelling.

The stonework on Highway 61 at Temperance River was built by an African-American forestry camp near Tofte. The camp had a brief existence, and local newspaper accounts indicate that here, as in many places in this pre-Civil Rights period, there was some discontent about having such a camp in the area.

Indian enrollees, Nett Lake Reservation, 1941

WPA rock quarry at Mendota, 1941

Minnesota Historical Society

Fort Snelling

The WPA opened a transient camp, the Mendota Camp, within the borders of what is now Fort Snelling State Park. This camp is notable since it is believed to be the only WPA camp within a state park to include African-American members.

This camp carried out a wide variety of tasks in the area, including road-grading, razing old buildings, constructing new buildings, and laying sewer lines. The WPA also had a hand in restoring historic Fort Snelling's Round Tower as a museum, with exhibits supplied by the Minnesota Historical Society.

On March 16, 1936, the African-American men at the camp staged a hunger strike, saying that the food served at the camp was poor. The superintendent launched an investigation, and the men went back to work. Just a few days later, most of the men in the camp were transferred to the Paul Bunyan Camp in Wabun, leaving only 36 behind.

Coming and Going

Camps saw a steady stream of men coming and going. Every six months, a large group would leave to be replaced with newcomers. Desertion was at first a small problem but became a major concern by the 1940s. Most deserters were young men suffering from homesickness.

Sometimes, entire companies of men were moved. The VCC camp that started at Sibley State Park moved on to Scenic State Park and finally Itasca State Park. Some camps were closed, and the men dispersed to other camps. Sometimes a group of men from one camp would be shifted to another until a larger project was completed.

While all the moving around gave the camps a temporary feel, for a few months or years, the camps were "Home, Sweet Home."

CCC camp buddies, Itasca State Park

MNDNR

FOUR

THE COLOSSAL COLLEGE OF CALLUSES: LIFE IN A CCC CAMP

A DAY IN THE LIFE OF A CCC CAMP

6:00 a.m.	Bugler Plays–Time to Wake Up
6:15	Exercises
6:30	Breakfast
7:15	Clean Up Camp and Check Out Tools
7:30	Roll Call and Inspection; Then Off to Work
11:15	Return from Work
Noon	Dinner
1:15 p.m.	Clean Up Camp
1:30	Check Out Tools
1:45	Back to Work
4:45	Return From Work
6:00	Supper
9:45	Lights Flashed
10:00	Lights Out
11:00	Bed Check

"This new life had a grip on me, and for the first time in months I was really happy. Good food, plenty of sleep, interesting work and genial companions had created quite a change–my mind was at peace."

–an enrollee

West wing of the mess hall at Ft. Ridgely State Park

Inside the barracks at Gooseberry Falls State Park

"The city slickers each chipped in five cents a week to one of the hardy natives, who was up at five and had a roaring fire going at six when we rolled out."

–an enrollee

MNDNR

Harold Vollbrecht

Emergency Relief Administration employees ready to leave for a day's work at St. Croix State Park, 1938

"If the inspector would find one cigarette butt, boy, I'll tell you, that taught you not to throw cigarette butts…two-thirds of the men smoked in camp, and if everyone threw cigarette butts, in a year's time you'd be knee-deep in cigarette butts."
—Harry Sperling, Itasca State Park

The day began in the pre-dawn hours when the night watchman or one of the enrollees lit fires in barrel stoves to warm up the barracks. As the buildings warmed up, a bugle would play reveille, and everyone would roll out. Beds were made, calisthenics done, and breakfast was served. After breakfast the entire camp was cleaned up.

"The mess hall contained about 20 wooden tables, each providing seating for ten men eating family style. A typical breakfast would always include coffee, milk, fruit, or juice and either cereal, pancakes and bacon, or scrambled eggs, toast and gravy. We were required to stand in place until the mess sergeant yelled 'Seats!' which was the signal to dive in." *—Frederick Johnson, Whitewater State Park*

J.F. Kieley

MNDNR

COMPANY 1723 C.C.C.—CAMP S

When it was time to work, the men were officially turned over to the project superintendent, assignments were given, and tools were checked out. Trucks carried groups of about 20 men to their jobs, and around the camp, blacksmiths, clerks, mechanics, and kitchen workers were at their tasks.

After a morning's work, it was lunch time: "They'd bring it out in cans and hot and sometimes these big milk cans, you know, we'd set them right in the fire to heat 'em up if they brought soup out there. We just set the cans right in the fire to heat the soup up. And if it was cold in the wintertime, if we had a fire going, we'd toast our sandwiches over a fire. Oh, that was really good." –*an enrollee*

After working the afternoon, the men would

Survey crew from Itasca State Park having lunch with Gust, the dog.

UGLAS LODGE, MINN. MARCH 15, 1935.

P.M.MEHL
MINNEAPOLIS.

Harry Sperling

return to camp where they'd have a chance to clean up, rest, or play basketball or softball. Just before supper, the bugle called the camp together for inspection and announcements. The flag was lowered, and the company was turned over to the Army once again.

After supper, enrollees could choose between resting, attending classes, or playing an organized sport. By 9:30 p.m. many were in bed, and most others would follow soon.

The Chow

By all accounts, there was plenty of food in the camps, although, in the words of one CCCer, "they didn't feed you what you liked, they fed you what was good for you."

"It always seemed, once a week, we had beef hearts. They'd buy these beef hearts and they'd slice them up and roast them and make them into gravy. We had good food. Skinny kids would come in and in six months they'd put on quite a few pounds–they'd fill out real good! It was always all you wanted to eat." –*Harley Heegard, Itasca State Park*

"Our cooks were often the targets of uncomplimentary remarks, made in an undertone so as not to invite retribution. I remember that the scrambled eggs had a distinct greenish cast, the pancakes had a texture similar to a cellulose sponge, great for soaking up syrup but tending to leave one with a heavy feeling. Of course, we were also served that mysterious mixture on toast that was probably part of the Army's discontent at Valley Forge." –*Frederick Johnson, Whitewater State Park*, in *Public Works*, October, 1980.

Company at retreat, Gooseberry Falls State Park

Hungry enrollees in chow line at Ft. Ridgely State Park

"They asked you to eat the food that you had on your plate, or don't take it. Either eat it or leave it alone. I know at the end of the month when the budget got a little tight, they'd set out six or eight big, ten gallon cans of Kool-Aid, or at that day called nectar. Of course, in hot weather everyone would try to fill up on something cool to drink, and of course, that way, just before dinner time, you wouldn't eat so much." –*Edward Schubert, Itasca State Park*

MNDNR

Don Price

Camp cooks at St. Croix State Park

After dinner at Gooseberry Falls State Park

MNDNR

Chicken dinner coming up, Sibley State Park

Games, Music, and Recreation

"Usually after dinner in the evening everybody would take off. Probably two or three of us would go out for a hike or something. Take off some deer trail and see how many deer we could see and so forth until it got dark and the mosquitoes got too bad, and we'd head back to camp." –*Edward Schubert, Itasca State Park*

"There was one fellow we called 'Birch Bark Stickney.' He was always making whistles. He was good at it. He had whistles of all sizes and descriptions and every tone you could think of. Whenever you heard that whistle you knew where Stickney was. When he was quiet, he was making a new whistle." –*Edward Schubert, Itasca State Park*

Many camps had musical ensembles: brass bands, string orchestras, choirs, accordion groups, and jug bands.

"We had a young Italian kid who was in the camp, John Tornina . . . He just loved to sing, 'O Sole Mio.' He had a good voice. You could hear him every evening. He'd be singing." –*Edward Schubert, Itasca State Park*

"The recreation hall usually contained a pool table, a few books and magazines. We had no radio, and TV was still a dream! A canteen was stocked with various items such as tobacco, candy, soft drinks, and toilet articles." –*Frederick Johnson, Whitewater State Park*

Striking up the band at the Cottonwood River Camp (Flandrau State Park)

A hot night of pool at the Cottonwood River Camp (Flandrau State Park)

Cribbage, whist, and penny ante poker for payday stakes were popular. "At ten o'clock the lights would go out, and then if you wanted to play poker all night, you had to play by candlelight. The poker players, they always had their candles handy. And they had to keep quiet too, otherwise there were guys that wanted to sleep. They were nice about it. You know, that poker game is terrible. It's an awful habit. You get into a game, you just don't want to quit, because if you are losing, you want to make your money back. Sometimes they'd play into the wee hours of the morning." –*Harry Sperling, Itasca State Park*

"We would sit around the woodstove, tell jokes, talk about girls, politics, and religion or read mail from home." —an enrollee

Harry Sperling

An evening in the barracks at Itasca State Park

"Well, it seemed like I never got bored, always had something to do. I didn't have any money. I had a lot of fun. Had a roof over my head. Had food, clothing, no worries." —Harley Heegard, Itasca State Park

Education

There were attempts to provide an educational program for enrollees throughout the New Deal. The success of these efforts was greater in official documents than it was in the memories of the enrollees. Some camps had more extensive programs where enrollees could earn high school credits. Others offered courses related to the work of the camp: welding, masonry, or safety.

It was sometimes claimed that all enrollees participated in education, but many accounts of the time say that it was optional. This may have varied from camp to camp: "Our only exposure to culture or education came in the form of debate teams which traveled from St. Mary's College in Winona to try out their arguments before a live audience. They also came to enjoy our food, which they claimed was far superior to that offered in their cafeteria."

–*Frederick Johnson*, *Whitewater State Park*

Whatever the participation level, even the official documents admitted that it was difficult to get good educational advisors and keep them in camp. After one year, the CCC had lost 50% of the original advisors, and retaining these workers was a perpetual problem. Their job was not only to provide classes and tutoring, but to advise each enrollee on a career path.

Some enrollees remember their CCC education with real pride. A good advisor was treated with honor. For many enrollees, the camp education program was a chance to "catch up." Thousands learned to read and write in camp.

The Education Building at Gooseberry Falls State Park

"Champs in 1940." Gooseberry Falls State Park CCC Camp baseball team

Sports

Probably all camps had at least informal games of baseball, basketball, or softball. In areas where there were other camps in proximity, leagues sprang up.

Frederick Johnson, Whitewater State Park, described a basketball game against a team from a nearby WPA transient camp: "You can imagine the makeup of the team we faced. The game was played in their recreation room, a building about the size of two boxcars placed side by side. We found their team to be short on finesse, but exceedingly long on strength. No fouls were called unless blood or bone was evident. I was not exactly as shifty as a windshield wiper, so I was fortunate to have as my individual opponent a gentle giant who apologized profusely for perspiring all over me as we caromed amiably off the walls and each other, being ever careful to avoid the hot coal stove on the sideline. I forget the score, I do remember that we won, and after the struggle, victor and vanquished shared a lunch of peanut butter sandwiches and coffee in the highest tradition of sportsmanship." (*Public Works*, October, 1980).

Basketball players for Whitewater State Park.
Frederick Johnson is the one in the middle.

Religious Services

One chaplain was assigned to cover several camps. There was usually an inter-denominational Protestant service once a week, along with a Catholic service led by a local priest.

Going to town or coming back to camp? Itasca State Park

Town, Cars, and Local Girls

"It was on a Sunday and we had dinner and then they had an orchestra there. A local girl came over and said, 'Do you want to dance?' I never had a woman ask me before, so I got up and danced with her. I went back to her later and I said, 'How's the chance to borrow your frame for the next struggle?' See, that was the saying at the time." *–Harley Heegard, Itasca State Park*

The men went to town (when there was one) for dances or parties on the weekends. Having an automobile at camp was forbidden, under penalty of being discharged, but it was still a common practice. The cars were hidden in the woods a short way from camp.

" . . . it had been raining and then freezing, so it was slippery. This friend of mine and this guy he was going to fight with, they went outside, and he hit my friend and knocked him down, and he slid under a Model A car. Model A cars are high, you know. And he crawled back out of there, and he got hit again, and he went back under there. Well, that stopped the fight then. It was no use fighting. He was up and down all the time." *–Harley Heegard, Itasca State Park*

Pranks

The camps were famous for practical jokes, pranks, and tom-foolery. There were no televisions or radios, and the men looked for ways to entertain themselves. Newcomers bore the brunt of the jokes. They would be ordered to water the flag-pole or undertake other nonsensical tasks. One of the favorite initiation rites for new enrollees was snipe hunting: "You take 'em out in the woods in the dark, and you give them a gunny sack, and you put them by some little place where the snipe would come through, and they'd stand there holding the sack, and then we'd go around we'd make a drive. And instead of going around making the drive, we'd head back to camp, and it was dark, and the poor guy, you know, we had lost one guy in the woods that way. We had the whole darn camp out looking for him . . . he was missing for about two or three hours . . . I'll tell you, there was no more snipe hunting after that." *–Harry Sperling, Itasca State Park*

Fooling around back at camp, Cottonwood River Camp (Flandrau State Park)

MNDNR

MNLINK

MNDNR

"You get a bunch of men together, and you give them free time, and there's going to be something happening!"
—an enrollee

Goofing off at Itasca State Park

"Well, one thing that they used to love to do was short sheet the bed. Then you'd try to get into bed, and of course, you'd get halfway and that was it. Horsehair was another thing. Somebody would get horsehair put in bed, and scratch and itch just something fierce." *—Edward Schubert, Itasca State Park*

"I can remember, the guys short-sheeted him. I think he came in a little bit under the bottle, and he stuck his feet right through the sheets. He just crawled in bed, stuck his feet through the sheets and made holes in the sheets, and he went to sleep. Everybody got quite a kick out of that."
—Harley Heegard, Itasca State Park

"There was one guy; he was from Hawley. I can't remember his name, but we called him 'Moon' . . . when we were getting our shots . . . everybody was lined up to go into the hospital where they give the shots. And, of course, I was always the crazy devil, you know, when I come out, I held my arm and I'd holler, you know, like it hurt, and I'd roll on the ground and you know, the guy passed out. He couldn't stand it. So . . . they come out, and they gave him his shot while he was passed out." *—Harry Sperling, Itasca State Park*

MNDNR

It was a long, long winter at St. Croix State Park

"We had one guy carrying icicles into the kitchen . . . the worst of it is, when you first come into camp and you meet a guy, he might be just an ordinary person, but he's dressed up in his army clothing. You don't know who he is, and he'll act like an army officer. And he says, 'Say, you, our electricity went out.' (It was the springtime of the year when the icicles were hanging off the roof.) He says, 'You pick [the icicles] all off and carry 'em and put 'em in the freezer' . . . And the poor guy, first of all they made him roll up his pants legs above his knees. He says, 'They won't let you in the kitchen unless you got your pants legs up.' And when he come into the kitchen, well, the guys in the kitchen didn't know what that was all about." –*Harry Sperling, Itasca State Park*

Special Events

Holidays were celebrated with special meals, and if they weren't too far from home, enrollees could get leave to be with their families. A certain number of men had to stay in camp, especially in camps that were on fire-watch during the dry 1930s.

The camp sent elaborate holiday cards and frequent communications to the families of enrollees. This was done to reassure the family that their son was in good hands, and it was seen as good, general public relations for the CCC.

Some camps put on pageants, plays, and skits. If the production was elaborate, the locals would be invited to attend.

THANKSGIVING

1937

COMPANY 2710
CCC

TWO HARBORS, MINNESOTA

— MENU —

Cream of Tomato Soup
Crackers

Curled Celery   Olives   Sliced Dill Pickles

Roast Young Turkey
Cranberry Sauce
Sage Dressing

Snowflake Potatoes
Giblet Gravy

Candied Sweet Potatoes

Creamed Carrots and Peas

Fruit Salad

Coffee

Mince Meat Pie

Mixed Candies

Cigarettes

Special menus for the holidays

A Merry Christmas and a Happy New Year to All
1935

CCC Christmas card from St. Croix State Park

Lingo

The men generated a multitude of slang words and jargon to go with camp life.
Each camp had its own collection.

THIS SUPPOSED DIALOGUE BETWEEN TWO CCCERS

is from the May 21, 1936 *Farmers Independent*, a newspaper
published in Bagley, Minnesota. A key to the slang follows:

"Hey, Greaseball, got a stiffy?"

"I've got some sawdust and blankets."

"Got a firestick?"

"Boy, you certainly need those dog kennels of yours for this mud, don't you?"

"Pontoons would be better."

"Yeah, I was on them today in the brush, and the snow was so soft, and I
stumbled so much, I just about went brush batty."

"See any pin-cushion squirrels?"

"Yeah, two of 'em."

"Must be time for chow; there goes the pill pusher after the Louie."

"Can you treat me to a bottle of slough water after chow?"

"Naw, won't even be over there; gonna hit the hayloft."

"You can't do that. The Sin-buster is talkin' tonight in the Rec Hall."

"Oh, oh, I forgot. Gimme your rake a second."

KEY

Brush Batty = crazy from working in the woods

Dog Kennels = shoes

Firestick = match

Greaseball = truck driver

Hayloft = bed

Louie = Lieutenant

Pill Pusher = doctor

Pin-cushion Squirrel = porcupine

Pontoons = snowshoes

Rake = comb

Sawdust and Blankets = tobacco and paper

Slough-water = soda pop

Sin-buster = clergyman

Stiffy = cigarette

MNDNR

"To take one's place among his fellow men and be accepted as a friend is a fine thing for any man."
                    —an enrollee

Friends at Whitewater State Park

FIVE

WE CAN TAKE IT: THE WORK PROJECTS

Stumps

I hope that I shall never see

A stump outside the CCC.

A stump whose wiry roots are found

Deep in the earth's tenacious ground.

A stump at which I slave away

All during a torrid summer day.

Stumps are dug by guys like me

And others in the CCC.

–from *Happy Days*, the CCC national newsletter

"We Can Take It" was the unofficial slogan of the CCC. The New Deal agencies took on an unprecedented amount and variety of work projects throughout Minnesota and America. Nicknames for the CCC included, "Roosevelt's Tree Army" and "The Soil Soldiers." These military metaphors allude to the only other example of such massive citizen mobilization and accomplishment.

A Bagley, Minnesota newspaper (*Farmer's Independent*, May 25, 1933) quoted CCC Director Robert Fechner as saying that the proposed 10-year forest protection program would be completed in just two years! At one time, it was estimated that the CCC planted over half of all the trees ever planted in the United States.

CCC work crew at Gooseberry Falls State Park

A FEW ACHIEVEMENTS OF THE CCC ON A NATIONAL SCALE

Trees planted:
2,356,000,000

Trails and roads constructed (in miles):
126,000

Telephone lines (in miles):
89,000

Fire fighting (in man-days):
6,459,000

Erosion control dams built:
6,660,000

Acres covered for plant disease and pest control:
21,000,000

—from a summary of the nine years of the CCC, by James J. McEntee, the last CCC Director

Hillside tree planting at Whitewater State Park

"The boys allowed on the job were between the ages of 17 and 22, and most of them, to begin with, were town boys that...didn't know the business end of an ax. Most of them were willing to learn, though, and everything went fine after we got started."
—Peter Gregorson, LEM for the NYA at Lake Bemidji State Park

Several factors came together to produce this unheard-of achievement. The nation had just been through the logging era, which created the need for massive reforestation. The National Park Service and the Forest Service had a backlog of projects that only needed more manpower to move forward. In the New Deal plans, in the government agencies that launched them, and in the spirit of the nation, there was a happy unity of purpose and resources that just plain worked.

Once the New Deal agencies were up and running, they created their own momentum. Each camp had 200 men who needed to work every day. Superintendents became experts at finding meaningful work. The early camps, that didn't have a backlog of projects or years of experience, just rolled up their sleeves and found something worthwhile to do. Al Salvaag, who worked at Lake Bemidji for the NYA, said that he and his co-workers received no formal training for their work. They just started in and learned on the job.

Some of the public perceived that the CCC, WPA, and NYA were "make-work" bureaus. However, there is very little, either in the accounts of the men who were there or in the detailed records that were kept, to indicate that there was much work that was cooked up just to keep people busy. They never ran out of work. Many projects were left unfinished when the agencies were shut down.

USFS

Learning to use an axe

A SAMPLING OF THE WORK DONE AT JUST ONE CAMP AT ITASCA INCLUDES:

- constructing log benches
- erecting signs
- trapping beaver
- counting deer
- staining existing buildings
- grading beds for pipelines
- planting trees
- moving rocks
- obliterating old roads
- fire suppression

- installing water lines
- pouring cement for floors
- conducting topographic surveys
- cleaning beach sand
- blasting rock
- milling lumber
- laying sod
- removing dead trees
- spraying for forest tent caterpillars

- sharpening tools
- razing old buildings
- brushing out currants and related species
- building cabinets
- erecting stone walls
- cutting firewood
- moving buildings
- stringing power lines

All of this work doesn't even include the buildings and other structures!

USFS

Testing water quality

Chopping firewood

The projects were described as "conservation work," and many of them were direct work in forests, or on erosion projects. "Infrastructure work" might have been a better phrase to describe the building of roads, bridges, water towers, utility lines, and other elements of the public systems that underl ay our lives.

Firefighting equipment

"Here's how we fought most of the fires. We had a five-gallon tank. It was kind of a flat tank that strapped on your back, and it had a little hand pump and you could really put out fires. Just think of taking twenty-five to thirty men with a tank like that. You can put out quite a fire if you can get near it…we had a little pump that they took down in the swamp, and they drove a little point down in, and then they'd hook the pump up to it, and they'd pump the water, and they'd pump it right into your tank and away you'd go."
—Harry Sperling, Itasca State Park

Fire Fighting

Fire fighting wasn't one of the original purposes of the New Deal agencies, but soon after the opening of the CCC, it happened that fires broke out in the vicinity of camps. Camp superintendents requested permission to use their men to help, and permission was granted. In those days, fighting fires was strictly a hand-to-hand, labor-intensive job, and the presence of 200 men could be a pivotal element in stopping a large fire.

Fire suppression quickly became one of the primary jobs of the CCC. Nationally, 47

CCC enrollees lost their lives fighting fires. During the drought years of the 1930s, a record number of fires were reported, but the acreage burned was the lowest ever in the U.S.

"We were knocking down brush and trees and digging a trench. We tried to keep the fire from spreading. It was hard work and long hours, and you come in so tired at night—you slept in hay barns—you went to sleep and didn't know anything."
—Harvey Richart, Gooseberry Falls State Park

Fighting a forest fire in the vicinity of Gooseberry Falls State Park

Tree planting at Gooseberry Falls State Park

Tree Planting

Much of the logging that was done in the late nineteenth and early twentieth centuries involved clear cutting. The remaining landscape, filled with dead limbs but few trees, was ripe for fires and extensive erosion. FDR had planted trees on his family's estate, and planting trees was surely one of the first projects he had in mind for the CCC.

Some of the tree planting has left us the regular rows of red pine that can be found throughout the state. In the western part of the state, shelterbelts of mixed species were planted to break the wind. Some of the park structures were developed with landscape plans that were detailed down to the individual tree.

Road Work

When a camp opened in a park and the enrollees had arrived, the first jobs would be brushing and grading roads or construction areas. The newcomers got an immediate taste of hard, dirty work. If it happened to be winter, the job might be done in extreme cold.

> *"I remember one time we was over by Ice Cracking Lake. We was building a road down an old railroad grade and Dick Wilson was our foreman...It seemed like he always walked ahead of us, motioning us on and stuff like that. So, we go moving along, and by kicking the throttle lever ahead I got more horsepower out of this Cat, so we was running along, and I hooked a popple tree. We jerked the grader right in half, right there."*
> —Harley Heegard, Itasca State Park

National Archives, 079-E4I-MN-SPI2-I5-PII66-NO43-1934

An unplanned "detour" during construction of the Ft. Ridgely State Park entrance road

These roads, parking lots, and campgrounds are part of the "invisible" legacy of the New Deal era. We use them, usually without a thought, but a lot of planning went into them when they were built. Prior to the 1930s, park development was minimal or haphazard. By concentrating and planning high-use areas, park designers could protect the beauty of these places and enhance the experience of park visitors.

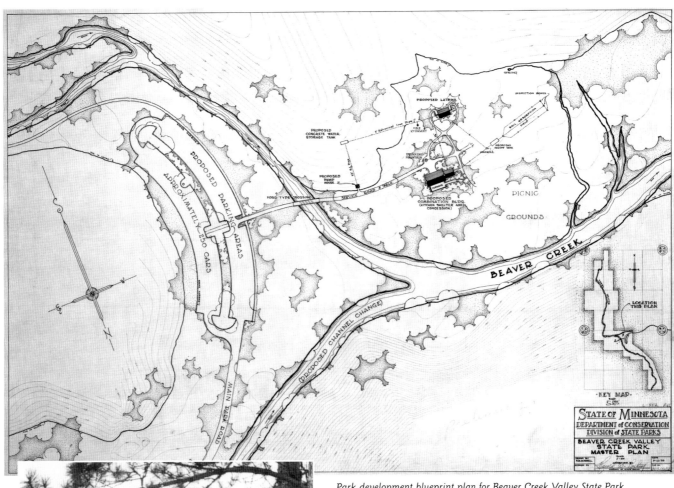

Park development blueprint plan for Beaver Creek Valley State Park

The St. Croix Recreational Development Area

The most extensive example of how planning shaped a park is at St. Croix State Park. St. Croix was Minnesota's only Recreational Demonstration Area (RDA). RDAs were formed by purchasing land that was less-than-ideal for farming and turning it into a park. At St. Croix, the result was the state's largest collection of New Deal buildings, clustered into several group camps that are still in use today (See page 105 for more details). One of the notable features of an RDA was the necessary cooperation of several agencies to accomplish the work.

*Original entrance sign
for St. Croix Recreational
Demonstration Area*

MNDNR

MNDNR

Forest pest tree inspection

Other Forest Work

White pine blister rust is a tree-killing fungus that first arrived in Minnesota's forests in 1908. Even to this day, it has thwarted efforts to regenerate white pine trees. To spread, blister rust requires a currant or gooseberry plant. It was hoped that by pulling up these plants where they were found near white pines in the forest, the trees could be saved. New Deal agencies eradicated currants from millions of acres, but the problem was too widespread for their efforts to make much of a difference.

Enrollees also sprayed insecticides to fight against forest tent caterpillars and other insects. They brushed out fire lines, and they logged for firewood and lumber for their building projects.

Work Planning

Each camp had a lot to do just to maintain itself. Kitchen workers, blacksmiths, educational advisors, and commanding officers continued their work as long as the camps were running. Every morning, the rest of the men would be divided into groups and sent off to their work sites. The commanding officer kept a "situation board" that had movable tags showing where each man was working. Then, if he was needed for something, or if his parents showed up for a surprise visit, the officer would know where to find him.

Agency publications, visits from officials, and daily announcements were used to foster a sense of how each enrollee's work contributed to "the Big Picture." For someone who just spent several days pulling currant bushes, it probably took some imagination to feel a part of the grand scheme. Testimony from the time, however, suggests that most enrollees did realize the scale of the movement of which they were a part.

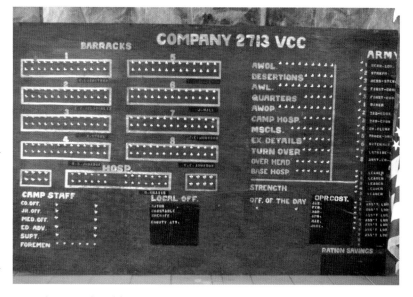

Original situation board from St. Croix State Park

"The CCC program was the best thing this nation ever had. The accomplishments that the men did could never be equaled again."
—Harvey Richart, Gooseberry Falls State Park

Construction of the castle wall for the concourse at Gooseberry Falls State Park

SIX

LOG AND STONE: THE BUILDINGS

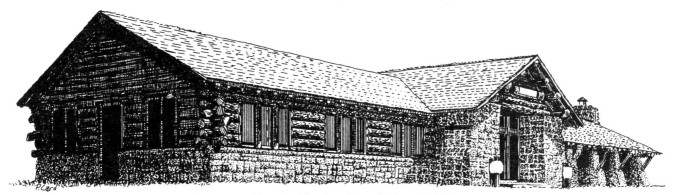

Sketch of Forest Inn from the "Itasca State Park Historic Buildings Tour" brochure. Drawn by Peter Card III, 1995

Rustic Style

Through the first decades of the twentieth century, the National Park Service developed a philosophy of design that became known as "Rustic Style." Among the first examples of this style was Old Faithful Inn at Yellowstone. The style featured the use of natural elements, specifically log and stone, and an attempt to harmonize structures with the surrounding landscape.

Rustic style architecture was a break from the prevailing styles of the time, which featured classical, stylized forms. The National Park Service made a concerted effort to implement rustic style in its own parks, and at the outset of the New Deal, trained architects in the individual states in the new style.

The Refectory, Gooseberry Falls State Park

EDWARD W. BARBER

Ed Barber was a young architect looking for a job when he signed on to work in what became the Minnesota Central Design Office. Throughout the New Deal era, he led the small group of architects, engineers, and draftsmen who churned out plans for the buildings that were springing up across the state. According to Judge Hella, Barber was behind every plan that came out of the Design Office, and these plans included the drawings for Forest Inn at Itasca, River Inn at Jay Cooke, the picnic shelters at Whitewater and Sibley, the shelter/pavilion at Scenic, and the buildings at Gooseberry, among other outstanding rustic masterpieces.

It is to Rustic Style that we owe the use of the local rock that gives such a singular flavor to the buildings and captures the particular spirit at different parks: the bright, airy feel of Whitewater, the subtle blend at Interstate, and the pinks of Sibley.

Building with Stone

The stone walls of buildings are perhaps one of the best-known legacies of the New Deal agencies. These practical monuments gave an "authorized" feel to the new parks, and since that time, millions of visitors have marveled at the strength and immensity of these walls.

"I remember the first day in the quarry. Our crew pusher asked if any of us could drive a truck. About ten hands went up. He pointed to some wheelbarrows and said, 'There's your truck, start loading them up with that stone and rock.'"
—Bob Glockner, CCC enrollee

Collecting stone for work projects, Gooseberry Falls State Park

Getting the rock in place

One of the biggest challenges in building with stone is getting the rocks to the work site and then up on the wall. The rocks in some of the walls were estimated to weigh as much as seven tons. Many projects had special derricks built for them. The crews also used hoists, levers and fulcrums, ramps, and out-and-out muscle to get the stones in place.

Rocks were selected for their shape to fit into the wall. The men would take metal coat hangers apart and bend them to fit the space for the next rock. Then they would take this template to the rock pile and start searching for a rock that was just right.

If the rock selected didn't naturally fit the space needed, it would have to be shaped. This was a slow, arduous process done with hammers and chisels, and one slip could mean starting all over again. Members of stone crews told of the large number of rocks that were rejected because they weren't perfect.

These crews didn't start out as expert stone masons. On more than one park building, it is possible to see that the stonework improved as the wall got higher and the crew benefited from practicing on the lower courses. In general, the WPA and VCC stone crews left the finest stonework. In the case of the WPA, the projects were often smaller scale and carried out over a longer time, which allowed for more care. Also, both the WPA and the VCC crews consisted of older, more experienced men.

Once the stonework part of a project was completed, the stone was given an acid bath, which removed any old cement wash, dirt, or discoloration. Then a carpentry crew would come in to build the roof and, in some cases, the entire upper section of the building.

The VCC crew at Ft. Ridgely State Park gets the custodian's residence ready for a roof

The Stone at Gooseberry Falls

The red and blue stones at Gooseberry Falls are among the most beautiful in the state. The red stone was from a quarry in Duluth near the College of St. Scholastica, and the darker, blue stone was quarried near East Beaver Bay. The stones were trucked from these locations back to camp.

Two Italian-Americans, John Berini and Joe Catanio, and a Swede, Axel Anderson, supervised the stonework at Gooseberry. The stone masons boasted that if all the mortar were removed from the walls the buildings would still stand.

The concourse along Highway 61 is one of the most formidable stone structures in the state. The size of the rocks used, the flowing lines of the courses, and the magnitude of the wall all add to its impressiveness. The park's blacksmith, Pete Mertes, built an enormous derrick with a 40-foot boom. The derrick stood at highway level and was used to shift cement, mortar, and rock down to the lower level and to lift stones up to the course in which they would be placed.

The concourse wall at Gooseberry Falls State Park nears completion

Ice and wood house at Scenic State Park, photo by Edward W. Barber.

Building with Logs

Another aspect of the New Deal architectural legacy is built out of wood. Gigantic, straight, close-grained logs grace many of the finest buildings in the state parks. These buildings arose from a time when such big logs for building were still available in the United States.

Sibley Speaks, the newsletter of the VCC camp at Sibley State Park, described how Burt Morton, a LEM who served as a foreman there, selected wood: "The park was combed thoroughly for suitable dry white oak. The logs had to scale to a certain size. They had to be just so long and straight as a die. No large knots or dry rot would be considered. All in all it was quite a task to find material that would measure up to Mr. Morton's specifications. Many a day was spent in his company, tramping over the park in an attempt to find exactly what he wanted. Red oak, bur oak, and scarlet oak would not do. Nothing but the straightest, soundest, and finest of white oak."

Logs were either taken from areas cleared for other purposes or felled specifically for their lumber. They were limbed and hauled to camp, where a sharp broad-ax or drawknife was used to shave and smooth the surface of the log. The rest of the fitting was done with axes or saws.

As with stones, one of the challenges of building with logs was getting them up into place. The crews used levers, hoists, harnesses, and manpower to get logs up to the tops of the walls. Often there was still work to be done there, filing and shaping the wood for a close fit.

Preparing logs for the Old Timer's Cabin, Itasca State Park

The Old Timer's Cabin at Itasca

One of the more striking examples of log building in state parks is the Old Timer's Cabin at Itasca State Park. It was one of the earliest CCC buildings, and the logs used were so thick that it only required four of them to make a wall. The National Park Service publication, *Park Structures and Facilities*, featured the Old Timer's Cabin as a noteworthy example of Rustic Style architecture. It included these comments: "Almost humorous in its scale, it is far from that as a reminder of magnificent forests all but extinct. As a relic of the days when trees were trees, this cabin can inspire us to firm resolution to permit them to be so again in the long term future."

One of the stirring impressions produced by these buildings is the thought that they could never be built again. The big trees are gone. There is still stone, but where would one find the crew that could work the stone on the scale of the 1930s? Modern architects and builders can make fine structures of a different sort, but the precise mix of rustic style and awe-inspiring size will live on only in the buildings that we still have from the New Deal era and the resonant echo of stories in log and stone.

The walls are up on the Old Timer's Cabin, Itasca State Park

The Old Timer's Cabin is finished and ready for two young visitors

MNUNR

View of the Old Timer's Cabin from Lake Itasca

EPILOGUE
WORLD WAR II AND THE END OF AN ERA

> *"What I learned in the CCC saved my butt in Europe many times."*
> *—Laudie Kacalek, Itasca*

CCC enrollees at Cottonwood River State Park (Flandrau)

Through the late 1930s, the New Deal agencies got smaller with each passing year. As the economy improved, it became more difficult to recruit and keep enrollees. The CCC was plagued with a high rate of desertion (20 percent by 1939).

Several factors combined to lessen the influence of the New Deal agencies: the novelty wore off, the number of agencies had multiplied so that no one agency could make the kind of splash the CCC had made at the beginning, the economy was improving, and FDR became more concerned with balancing the federal budget.

Hanging over the world in the 1930s was the threat of Adolf Hitler's Nazi regime. As Americans became more nervous about their own defense, they were less likely to object to the militarization of the New Deal agencies, and quasi-military training was added to all of them by the early 1940s. It has been said that the experience gained from being in a New Deal work camp helped prepare a generation of Americans for war.

Parade in military dress at Gooseberry Falls State Park

As early as 1937, the Roosevelt Administration had tried, without success, to make the CCC a permanent agency. By 1939, continued efforts to make the CCC permanent were going nowhere. Critics of the agency finally surfaced, and the need for soldiers in the war reduced support for the CCC. On June 5, 1942, the House of Representatives voted, 158-151, not to appropriate any more money for the agency, but instead, to provide $500,000 for its liquidation.

FDR and his Cabinet

The legislation to end the CCC then went to the Senate, where 32 senators voted to retain the CCC, 32 voted to withhold its appropriation, and 32 didn't vote. A second vote resulted in another tie, and Vice President Henry Wallace broke the tie by upholding the CCC. However, in the conference committee, it became obvious that the House would not compromise, and on June 30, 1942, the CCC and VCC came to an end. The NYA and WPA lasted on into the next year but then met the same fate.

The Legacy of the New Deal Agencies

During its life span of nine years, 2.5 million Americans

Homeless in Minneapolis park

Log and stone construction at Gooseberry Falls State Park, Campground Shelter

passed through the CCC. The unprecedented mobilization that took place as the United States entered World War II was aided by experience gained in the New Deal agencies. It is generally agreed that the New Deal itself did not pull the country out of economic hard times (that happened during World War II). However, there is no doubt that the New Deal meant survival to millions of Americans during the Great Depression.

The CCC, WPA, and NYA helped improve civic life in the 1930s. Both New York City and Chicago reported reductions in crime of almost 50 percent in the years following the beginning of the New Deal and attributed it to the CCC. The VCC pacified World War I veterans who were angry about how things had turned out for them in the years since the war.

The annual cost per CCC enrollee was just over $1000; for the WPA, it was around $800, and for the NYA, $400 to $700. James McEntee, who had become the second director of the CCC after the death of Robert Fechner, figured that the economic value of all the work projects done amounted to $664

per enrollee, and of course, that doesn't include the use that we still get from some of the structures.

It is the value that we get today from the work of the New Deal agencies that makes their legacy such a remarkable story. The national, state, and local park systems of today are unimaginable without the groundwork of the New Deal. The growth of parks during that period dwarfs later expansions. From the inventory and selection of sites for parks, to the planning and design, to the splendid log and stone structures, the work of subsequent decades has built on what happened in the 1930s and early 1940s.

Could the CCC, VCC, WPA or NYA work again? There have been similar versions in the past few decades, but the difference in scale makes it difficult to compare efforts such as the Job Corps or the Minnesota Conservation Corps with the New Deal work programs. Probably it would take a major socioeconomic event like the Great Depression to create the political conditions necessary to bring about another such civilian mobilization.

After World War II, the United States was a different country. The new prosperity and the explosion of the automobile age meant that families could take vacations farther from home. In Minnesota, the CCCers and other New Deal workers brought their families back to the parks to see their handiwork. Visiting the parks "where Dad worked" became a family tradition. The faithfulness of these men and their families sustained Minnesota's state parks and helped fashion the places they have become.

In all of the stories from the now old men who served in the New Deal agencies, none are broadly critical of the experience. Certainly there were specific complaints: the food, the cold, the hard work; but these reservations are always tinged with respect. These men are glad they were there, and they have fond memories of the rugged life, the sense of accomplishment, the skills learned, and above all, the camaraderie.

Their attitude is expressed in Director Robert Fechner's 1936 Christmas greeting to CCC enrollees: "You have only to look at each other to appreciate the benefit that has accrued to each enrollee in renewed health, in new interest in new life, in reawakened desires of education and job perfection, and in rekindled ambition, to understand the full measure of the CCC's contribution to its enrollees. But it is not necessary for you to look even so far afield as your neighbor to realize these things, for each one of you has had a hand in one of the most gigantic projects the American government has ever undertaken. You are participating in the greatest conservation movement the country has ever known and as a direct result of this participation you have gained a revitalized outlook on life."

Camping at Scenic State Park

> *"The intangible benefits of the CCC to its members and society are greater than its material accomplishments."*
> *–Lee Evans, VCC Company 2713, Ft. Ridgely State Park*

CCC gravel crew, 1938. Gooseberry Falls State Park

MNDNR

Harry Sperling with camp mascot, Gust, at Itasca State Park

"IF I COULD STILL SIGN UP, I'D STILL SIGN UP."

—Harry Sperling, Itasca State Park, in 1993

Leaving camp, Company 2703, Itasca State Park

"They were the best years of my life."

Frank Cuzzi, from Duluth, on the accordion at Jay Cooke State Park. Music played an important role in camp life. Enrollees who could play an instrument were invaluable to camp morale (provided they had talent).

Log rolling demonstration on the Gooseberry River, Gooseberry Falls State Park. Sharing their expertise and participating in local activities provided good public relations and helped give the enrollees a sense of community.

A WPA Nature Guide is stationed at the Headwaters in Itasca State Park to give out information and answer questions. Interpretive services in Minnesota State Parks began in 1941 in cooperation with the University of Minnesota and the Minnesota Works Projects Administration.

HERE 1475 FT. ABOVE THE OCEAN THE MIGHTY MISSISSIPPI BEGINS TO FLOW ON ITS WINDING WAY 2552 MILES TO THE GULF OF MEXICO

Hughes Collection

MNDNR

Hughes Collection

Winter recreation at Gooseberry Falls State Park. Sports such as tobogganing, hockey, skiing, snowshoeing and even bob-sledding made the long winters in camp easier to bear.

Workers take a break to pose for the camera at Whitewater State Park. While there were staff photographers hired to document the projects, enrollees often took candid snap-shots or posed for each other. These are the images that truly capture the memories of life in the work camps.

MNDNR

THE LEGACY OF THE PARK BUILDERS

Blacksmith shop at St. Croix State Park

You can still experience the New Deal Era in Minnesota State Parks. You can see for yourself the rich colors in the stonework, feel the texture of the rock, smell the wood smoke of fires from the past, and listen with an imaginative ear for echoes from the 1930s.

SAMPLE THE HIGHLIGHTS OF THE NEW DEAL LEGACY BY VISITING THESE STATE PARKS:

- The German-style architecture at **Flandrau** State Park

- The exquisite color and quality of the stonework at **Gooseberry** Falls State Park

- The way the native basalt used at **Interstate** State Park blends with the surrounding rock

- At **Itasca** State Park, the historic feel of Forest Inn; the natural look of the carefully constructed stepping-stones at the Headwaters of the Mississippi and the chance to sleep in a New Deal Era cabin

- The stately beauty of River Inn and the excitement of the Swinging Bridge at **Jay Cooke** State Park

- The engineering of the dam project at **Lake Bronson** State Park

- The Yellowbanks CCC Camp outdoor exhibit at **St. Croix** State Park and the sheer number of period buildings

- The craftsmanship of the Shelter/Pavilion log work at **Scenic** State Park

- The well-preserved, exacting stonework at **Sibley** State Park

- The airy feel of the limestone architecture and the splendid picnic shelter at **Whitewater** State Park

---

Part II is a guide to the structures remaining from the New Deal Era. Here you'll find a section for each of the 27 parks that still have a New Deal Era legacy that you can see. These structures were built so well that most of them are still standing. Some that were intended to be "temporary" are still in use!

Part II will help you discover and understand the New Deal legacy at each park. It can also help you plan your park visits.

Visiting Itasca State Park. East contact station.

PLANNING TRIPS TO NEW DEAL STATE PARKS

This section offers suggestions for trips around Minnesota to see more than 400 remaining New Deal Era structures. For park locations, see the map on the next page.

Day Trips

Descriptions of individual parks are organized regionally. If your starting point is within the region, you can reach all of the region's parks in a day. However, in most of the regions, one day won't give you nearly enough time to drive to all the parks to experience the New Deal treasures. If you only have one day, look through the park descriptions and choose one or two parks to visit in that day.

Itasca and St. Croix State Parks are so large and the structures so many and widespread that, unless you're just hitting the highlights, you'll need several days to see everything.

Gooseberry Falls, Whitewater, and Flandrau State Parks have a lot to see, but the structures are fairly close together and easy to find. You might manage it in one day, if you devote the whole day to a particular park.

Each of the other parks can be seen in one day, depending, of course, on your travel time and how thoroughly you want to experience them. Many of the state parks offer brochures and displays on the New Deal legacy where you can learn more.

The Grand Tour

Reading about the New Deal era will give you new eyes for your visits. If you want to see all of the outstanding structures remaining in the parks, you can do it in one, large "circle" around the state.

It would be possible to do the Grand Tour in two to three weeks. It all depends on how much time you spend at each park and at points in between. To make the complete circle, you would drive around 2,000 miles.

The fun of a grand tour is the experience of seeing the panorama of all that was accomplished between 1933-1943. The connections and contrasts between parks, styles, and settings will be especially clear. A New Deal Grand Tour also provides a nice sampler of Minnesota's state parks. All of the parks feature beautiful natural settings, and seeking out these historic buildings gives you a good excuse to visit them.

MAP OF MINNESOTA STATE PARKS WITH NEW DEAL ERA STRUCTURES AND MILEAGE CHART

Mileage Chart

From \ To	Old Mill	Lake Bronson	Scenic	Itasca	Lake Bemidji	Jay Cooke	Gooseberry Falls	Charles A. Lindbergh	Lake Carlos	Sibley	Lac Qui Parle	Interstate	St. Croix	Minneopa	Flandrau	Fort Ridgely	Camden	Lake Shetek	Blue Mounds	Whitewater	Temperance River	Cascade River	Judge C.R. Magney	Monson Lake	Split Rock Creek	Beaver Creek Valley	St. Paul
Buffalo River	116	152	196	91	127	218	268	133	102	145	141	236	240	256	236	209	194	212	241	333	308	327	351	134	223	367	233
Old Mill		39	180	120	121	264	296	222	190	264	257	353	355	377	357	324	309	327	360	448	346	366	390	253	342	484	347
Lake Bronson			196	136	137	280	312	238	206	280	273	369	371	393	373	340	325	343	376	464	362	382	406	269	358	498	363
Scenic				111	88	115	182	144	201	218	277	198	177	317	330	332	301	316	351	321	187	207	231	231	340	355	219
Itasca					41	150	204	105	44	137	199	231	213	236	256	211	223	238	275	326	249	269	293	148	263	360	222
Lake Bemidji						151	194	121	131	173	235	238	198	260	241	243	259	274	311	362	234	254	278	184	299	396	258
Jay Cooke							51	123	164	173	224	112	70	216	230	232	252	268	303	234	91	111	135	183	291	270	133
Gooseberry Falls								174	220	124	275	163	121	267	281	283	303	319	354	285	40	60	84	234	342	321	184
Charles A. Lindbergh									58	71	132	107	105	140	121	124	160	174	211	214	214	234	258	85	198	250	112
Lake Carlos										64	85	154	160	171	152	128	137	151	187	249	260	280	304	53	175	285	145
Sibley											60	124	126	118	99	73	88	102	138	214	164	184	208	11	126	250	114
Lac Qui Parle												176	177	115	96	86	60	74	111	228	315	335	359	50	99	264	142
Interstate													63	125	136	139	200	215	252	142	203	223	247	135	239	178	41
St. Croix														168	181	184	206	220	257	185	161	181	205	137	246	221	84
Minneopa															21	45	103	96	141	110	307	327	351	128	128	146	85
Flandrau																25	85	71	125	129	121	341	365	109	112	165	100
Fort Ridgely																	81	73	120	155	323	343	367	83	106	191	101
Camden																		29	52	211	343	363	387	92	39	247	160
Lake Shetek																			53	204	359	379	403	107	43	240	175
Blue Mounds																				229	394	414	438	144	19	265	237
Whitewater																					325	345	369	213	254	50	99
Temperance River																						20	44	274	382	361	224
Cascade River																							24	294	402	381	244
Judge C.R. Magney																								318	426	405	268
Monson Lake																									131	249	123
Split Rock Creek																										290	264
Beaver Creek Valley																											135

Parks in red contain New Deal-era buildings

Garden Island Recreation Area
Zippel Bay
Lake Bronson
Hayes Lake
Franz Jevne
Old Mill
Big Bog Recreation Area
Red River Recreation Area
McCarthy Beach
Soudan Underground Mine
Grand Portage
Judge C. R. Magney
Scenic
Cascade River
Bear Head Lake
Temperance River
Lake Bemidji
Hill Annex Mine
George H. Crosby Manitou
Tettegouche
Itasca
Schoolcraft
Split Rock Lighthouse
Gooseberry Falls
Savanna Portage
Jay Cooke
Buffalo River
Maplewood
Cuyuna Country Recreation Area
Moose Lake
Glendalough
Crow Wing
Banning
Lake Carlos
Mille Lacs Kathio
Father Hennepin
St. Croix
Charles A. Lindbergh
Big Stone Lake
Glacial Lakes
Wild River
Sibley
Interstate
Monson Lake
Lake Maria
Lac qui Parle
William O'Brien
Upper Sioux Agency
MPLS/ST. PAUL
Afton
Minnesota Valley Recreation Area
Frontenac
Camden
Fort Ridgely
Nerstrand Big Woods
Flandrau
Lake Shetek
Sakatah Lake
Carley
John A. Latsch
Minneopa
Rice Lake
Split Rock Creek
Whitewater
Great River Bluffs
Kilen Woods
Blue Mounds
Myre-Big Island
Beaver Creek Valley
Forestville/Mystery Cave
Lake Louise

DNR Information Center

651-296-6157

1-888-MINNDNR (MN toll free)

Telecommunications for the Deaf

651-296-5484 or 1-800-657-3929 (MN toll free)

DNR Web Site

www.dnr.state.mn.us

Minnesota State Parks With Remaining New Deal Structures

Much of the information included here is from the excellent work done by Rolf Anderson for the National Register of Historic Places Nominations and can be found in his "Final Report: Minnesota CCC/WPA Rustic Style Resources," 1988. Mr. Anderson's research has also recently been adapted and placed on the Minnesota Historical Society (MHS) website at **www.mnhs.org/places/nationalregister/stateparks/**.

The MHS website (**www.mnhs.org**) is an outstanding resource for anyone interested in learning more about any aspect of Minnesota history. For those needing information on the natural history features and recreational opportunities found in Minnesota's state parks, visit the Minnesota State Park's web pages at the Minnesota Department of Natural Resources website at **www.dnr.state.mn.us**.

Parks containing structures still visible from this era are organized below by region. Those with substantial New Deal period collections are listed in bold text. Parks that have limited evidence remaining but still have significant stories are included in a separate section entitled, "Contributing Park Collections."

NORTHWEST
Buffalo River (WPA)
Old Mill (WPA)
Lake Bronson (WPA)

NORTH CENTRAL
Scenic (CCC)
Itasca (CCC, WPA)
Lake Bemidji (NYA)

NORTHEAST
Jay Cooke (CCC, WPA)
Gooseberry Falls (CCC)

WEST CENTRAL
Charles A. Lindbergh (WPA)
Lake Carlos (WPA)
Sibley (VCC)
Lac Qui Parle (WPA)

EAST CENTRAL
Interstate (WPA)
St. Croix (CCC, WPA, VCC)

MINNESOTA RIVER PARKS
Minneopa (WPA)
Flandrau (CCC, WPA)
Fort Ridgely (CCC, VCC)

SOUTHWEST
Camden (VCC, WPA)
Lake Shetek (WPA)
Blue Mounds (WPA)

SOUTHEAST
Whitewater (CCC, WPA)

CONTRIBUTING PARK COLLECTIONS
Temperance River (CCC)
Cascade River (CCC)
Judge C.R. Magney
Monson Lake (VCC, WPA)
Split Rock Creek (WPA)
Beaver Creek Valley (WPA)

PARKS IN THE NORTHWEST

Buffalo River State Park

Buffalo River State Park was established in 1937. The original construction in the park, carried out by the WPA, included a bathhouse, staff residence, a latrine, a dam, and a swimming beach.

All of the WPA structures, which were constructed from local split stone, remain.

Buffalo River State Park Beach House and Pool

Old Mill State Park

Old Mill State Park was established in 1937. The name draws attention to the 1889 gristmill located in the park. The original WPA structures, still in use, were built at a cost of $11,000.

The area that became Old Mill State Park was used for recreation prior to 1937. After becoming a state park, it grew in popularity. An old-fashioned creamery picnic in 1938 drew more than 10,000 people.

The New Deal legacy in this park includes a shelter building, latrine, beach house, drinking fountain, dam, swimming beach, suspension bridge, and water tower. These split-stone structures were carefully designed to blend with the landscape.

The spillway for the diversion dam was removed in 2000 to improve the natural fishery of the river.

Stone suspension bridge at Old Mill State Park

Bronson Dam at Lake Bronson State Park

*Construction of the dam showing the pipes that remove
water from the saturated sand beneath the dam.*

Lake Bronson State Park

Lake Bronson State Park was established in 1937. After experiencing both drought and flooding during the early Depression years, the addition of a reservoir was intended to maintain a water supply, help control flooding, and meet the need for recreation.

Even after the plan to develop the dam was proposed, it was difficult to raise enough money to carry out the ambitious project. Eventually, appeals to Governor Floyd B. Olson and St. Paul banker and brewer, Adolph Bremer, who was a friend of President Roosevelt, resulted in the project being funded and completed.

The park still contains twelve structures built by members of a WPA transient camp. The facilities include a group camp mess hall, bath house, latrine, picnic shelter, office and garage, drinking fountains, a water tower, the foundation of the wash house from the WPA camp, the Lake Bronson dam, and Lake Bronson itself.

The Lake Bronson Dam project was even more difficult to carry out than anticipated, because saturated sand over 100' deep was discovered at the construction site. A system was designed by which the weight of the dam itself forced water up and out of the sand through 6-inch pipes. This "dried" the soil enough to support the weight of the dam. The pipes can still be seen in the dam tunnel.

As many as 350 people worked on the dam at any one time. Along with the other difficulties of the job, the mosquitoes were so thick that a number of horses were reported to have died from infections caused by inhaling them. The dam was completed in 14 months. It was the largest WPA project undertaken in Minnesota and remains one of the most impressive engineering achievements in the entire state park system.

The Water Tower, built in 1939, has both inner and outer walls and features an observation deck. The brick inner wall runs the full height of the building and it encloses the water tank (5,234 gallons) and pump. The outer wall is reinforced concrete faced with split fieldstone. The stairway to the observation platform winds up between the inner and outer walls.

The National Park Service designed this park "from the ground up." The service planned, defined, and organized the high-use areas along the shores of the new Lake Bronson.

MNDNR

Lake Bronson water tower

NORTH CENTRAL PARKS

Log maintenance building at Scenic State Park

Scenic State Park

Scenic State Park has an impressive collection of New Deal era log buildings. These include a shelter pavilion, naturalist's cabin, comfort station, shelter and latrine, water tower, custodian's cabin, equipment building, tool building, and an ice and wood house.

Land for Scenic State Park was first purchased in 1921, but development didn't begin by the CCC until 1933. They began work on June 21st, 1933, which made it the first CCC state park camp in Minnesota. The camp continued its work until January 1936. The nearby Link Lake forestry CCC camp finished several leftover projects.

Hugo Zaiser, who had been in charge of the park since it was established, became the camp superintendent. In addition to the regular CCCers, he headed a complement of eleven technical staff. The camp was housed at the south end of the park, near the present group camp on Lake of the Isles.

The buildings at Scenic are notable because they were the first complete collection of CCC structures built in the state. The residence and maintenance buildings are the only such buildings in the state built completely of logs.

The highlight at Scenic, even among so many fine buildings, is the shelter pavilion, built in 1934-1935. It sits on a concrete foundation faced with split stones. The walls were made of 10" logs and feature saddle-notched corners. The fireplace is made of stone, as is the terrace. The entrance is in the center of the east wall and consists of two plank doors with strap hinges.

Once you've admired the outside of the building, step inside to see one of the finest CCC interiors in the state park system. The tables and benches, made of split logs and log slabs, the log seats with branches used for backs, and the

Shelter Pavilion which has also been known as the Scenic State Park Lodge and as the Refectory Cabin

tables crafted from giant tree trunks were all built by the CCC under the supervision of Ole Evensen, a local experienced man (LEM).

Inside you'll also find a miniature woodland scene (including carved and painted trees, plants, and animals) in a glass case with a log frame. Hanging in the north gable, you'll see three images of a forest before, during, and after a fire painted by CCC enrollee, William Lewis.

Sometimes an enrollee left his personal mark on a building. Above the door of the bathroom building near the shelter, a pair of dice are embedded in the wall.

This may be the best spot in the state to let your imagination take you back to the 1930s–back to the time when camps bustled with the activity and creativity of young men working hard to make something of themselves and of the parks put in their care.

> *A classic book about park structures,* Park Structures and Facilities, *by Albert H. Good, written in 1935, testifies to the quality of the workmanship in the Scenic shelter building: "In this example Minnesota justifies her advantage of superior native timber resources by the fine character of the log construction … An imagined ideal park structure … would surely specify logs and log construction from Minnesota."*

Itasca State Park

Itasca State Park was established in 1891 and, in contrast to most other state parks, had fairly extensive development before the New Deal era. Douglas Lodge was built between 1905 and 1907. The Clubhouse was built in about 1911, and the old headquarters (now a hostel) and the Itasca Museum were built in the 1920s. Still, the extensive New Deal development here changed the face of Itasca, and left an impressive collection of 70 structures.

Several New Deal camps worked at Itasca. CCC Camp SP-1 was the first state park camp *approved* in Minnesota. It was *established* on June 27, 1933, just six days after the camp at Scenic State Park. In 1937, this camp was moved to the area that is today the Pine Ridge Campground and was renamed SP-19. The new men arriving at SP-19 had already built the log

buildings at Scenic State Park and the stone buildings at Sibley State Park. Perhaps finest among their many accomplishments at Itasca was the completion of Forest Inn. SP-19 was also notable as the last CCC state park camp in the United States, closing on July 15, 1942.

The Annex Camp (S-70), located near the Itasca east entrance, did roadwork, telephone line construction, tree planting, and fire fighting. When the camp closed, it was moved to Lanesboro, Minnesota, to work on erosion control.

The Lovelis Lake Camp (S-57) was located just west of the southwest corner of the park. A stone fireplace remains at the site. This camp built over 100 miles of forest road, three complete forestry headquarters facilities, and conducted other forestry work. One of the superintendents of this camp was

Forest Inn, Itasca State Park

> "One day an inspector from the Cities came up and asked old George Wilson what kind of a weather is it that you can't go out and work. 'How bad does the weather have to be?' He says, 'We don't have that kind of weather.' That meant that we'd go out regardless of how bad, if it was stormy or what, we always went. Never ever stayed in camp."
>
> —Harry Sperling, Itasca State Park

George "Haywire" Wilson, a lumberjack who was renowned both for his vigorous completion of tasks and for ignoring the many bureaucratic letters and memos that were sent to him.

Two WPA transient camps worked in Itasca, one at Lake Ozawindib and the other at Elk Lake, both sites of group camps in use today. One of the duties assigned to these two camps was to build Wilderness Drive, a ten-mile, scenic route, which they accomplished using only picks, shovels, and pails.

To visit the many New Deal sites at Itasca, you'll need a park map and plenty of time. Here's a list of highlights.

Highlights Among New Deal Era Structures at Itasca
The Mississippi Headwaters Dam

What visitor to Itasca has not photographed the Headwaters of the mighty Mississippi River? Before the New Deal, this picturesque spot was a swampy creek-mouth, but the CCC transformed it into the pleasing place it is today.

The CCC placed the exquisite stepping-stones and the little dam that creates rills between the stones here in 1934. The crew cleared some vegetation from the area and constructed a concrete dam below the water level. According to the original plans: "Before cement hardens, stone and pebbles [should be] pressed into the surface, making it appear as natural as possible. All exposed rock will be weathered and darkened."

This project was clearly a success, for the perfect ambiance of the spot has contributed to securing its place as one of the most important landmarks in the state.

Forest Inn and Nearby Buildings

One of the most impressive buildings in the state park system, Forest Inn was built between 1938 and 1940. It was intended to replace an older, smaller Forest Inn that was located in the present-day Douglas Lodge parking lot. The new Forest Inn required 7,100 man-days of labor and $9,602.66 for materials.

Some of the stone for construction of Forest Inn came from within the park, and some from quarries in the St. Cloud area. The logs came from the Chippewa National Forest, 80 miles east of Itasca. Forest Inn, with overall dimensions of 144' x 50', is one of the largest New Deal era buildings in Minnesota.

The interior originally had a snack area (refectory) in the center, a souvenir store in the north wing, and rest rooms and

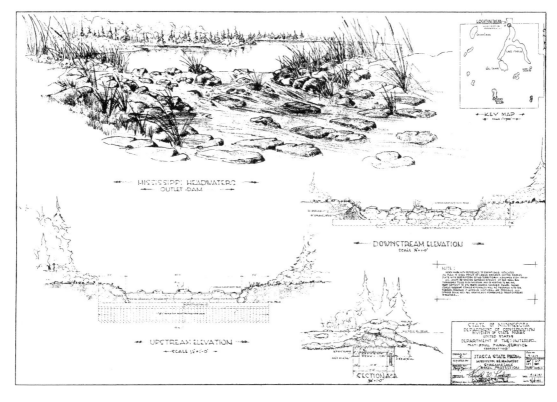

Architectural drawing for the Headwaters dam, Itasca State Park

Interior of Forest Inn shortly after completion

a meeting room with a split stone fireplace in the south wing. The refectory is gone, but the rest of the building is still used in the same way it was in 1940. One of the most impressive features of Forest Inn is the immense log truss system in the ceiling. Log light fixtures adorn the interior.

The stone crew included about 30 men who had worked on the stone buildings at Sibley State Park. Ole Evensen, from Scenic State Park, supervised the log work.

Several other New Deal era buildings at Itasca, notably the Fourplex, now called the Fireplace Rooms, built in 1937, stand near Forest Inn. While you're here, pick up the Historic Building Tour brochure to learn more about Itasca's architecture.

Old Timer's Cabin

This cabin features logs so thick that only four were needed to

make the height of a wall. Footings for the cabin were dug in the dead of winter, and by late April, the log structure was in place. By July 20th, the cabin was finished. The Old Timer's Cabin and Cabin 12 (across the lake from the Old Timer's Cabin) were the first two New Deal buildings at Itasca.

Sleeping in a New Deal Era Building

Several of the cabins still offered for rent at Itasca were built in the 1930s. The cabins have been modernized, but they still have the rustic feel provided by stone and logs.

In addition to the structures detailed above, Itasca State Park contains over 70 New Deal projects still visible today. For more information on Itasca's New Deal legacy, stop by Itasca's Jacob V. Brower Visitor Center or check out the Minnesota Historical Society website listed at the start of this section.

Cabin 12 in the Douglas Lodge area of Itasca State Park. Lodging reservations are recommended.

Lake Bemidji State Park

Though the park was established in 1923, development did not begin until 1938. The CCC camp at Itasca State Park provided some assistance, but the projects at Lake Bemidji (a shelter building and a sanitation building) were constructed by the National Youth Administration (NYA). These are the only buildings in the state park system built by the NYA.

The shelter building, completed in 1939, stands on the sandy shore of Lake Bemidji. It is a T-shaped building featuring log walls with saddle-notched corners. The main shelter area contains a stone fireplace with a beautiful split log mantel. Four cast-iron cook stoves can be found in the kitchen area. The cook stoves are original as are the windows and plank doors. The design of the building is identical to the shelter at Charles A. Lindbergh State Park.

Lake Bemidji State Park shelter building

NORTHEASTERN PARKS

Jay Cooke State Park

Named for the financier who helped fund the Army of the North during the Civil War, Jay Cooke State Park was established in 1915 with the donation of a parcel of land along the St. Louis River.

The design for development in the park, provided by the National Park Service, helped concentrate intensive use into manageable areas.

Development began in a small way when an Emergency Conservation Work force established several small picnic areas along Highway 210. Big changes began when CCC camp SP-2 was established on June

The Swinging Bridge spans the St. Louis River at Jay Cooke State Park

22, 1933. This camp worked on the Swinging Bridge and began development in the picnic grounds. It also undertook soil erosion projects, mainly directed at keeping Highway 210 (historic Skyline Drive) in passable condition. This camp was one of three in Minnesota that was to close before it had time to complete its work. The CCC camp from Knife River finished some of the remaining projects, including the Oldenburg Point Picnic Shelter.

In 1939, a second CCC camp opened. They continued work on the Swinging Bridge, built River Inn, and finished projects begun by camp SP-2. Camp SP-21 closed on March 25, 1942, near the end of the CCC era. The WPA continued work on roads in the park.

The buildings at Jay Cooke use black Duluth gabbros of different types, along with some granite trim from St. Cloud. Remaining New Deal structures in the park include River

River Inn, Jay Cooke State Park

Swaying on the Swinging Bridge, Jay Cooke State Park

MNDNR

Inn, the Swinging Bridge, and, in the Oldenburg Point Picnic Area, a shelter, a water tower/latrine building, and a drinking fountain. A custodian's cabin and a pump house are in the service yard area. At the site of the CCC camp, an oil tank, a latrine, and a few foundations are all that remain.

River Inn was built late in the New Deal period (1940-1942). It is one of the largest New Deal buildings in the state park system (123' x 48'). It was intended to be a combination building, with a shelter, rest rooms, a concession area, a dining room, and kitchen (one of few in the state). The shelter section contains a large stone fireplace and features heavy timber trusses. There are large, wrought iron hinges on the doors, and large, iron and timber chandeliers made by CCC blacksmiths. The riverside of the shelter has a stone terrace with a low stone wall. The north side has a smaller porch with a roof that is held up by three round, stone pillars.

The concession area was located to the east of the shelter. Originally, it had counter windows opening into the shelter and onto the terrace. In 1983, the kitchen and dining areas were remodeled into offices and space for interpretive exhibits.

The Swinging Bridge is 200' long, spanning the St. Louis River. The bridge hangs from two enormous piers made of reinforced concrete faced with slate taken from the river. The suspension cables are secured in concrete on the north side of the river and into rock on the south. The original walkway was made of 2" white oak flooring, with peeled cedar logs as railings.

The St. Louis River watershed drains a large part of northeastern Minnesota, and the force of the river during the spring and early summer run-off is astounding. The bridge was originally built 18' above the river, but the deck washed out frequently during the 1930s. The deck height was increased in 1941 by the second CCC camp, and again in 1953, when the piers had to be raised to get the walkway even higher.

The first CCC camp built the water tower/latrine building in the Oldenburg Point Picnic Area in 1934. The latrine portion of the building has 18" thick stone walls, 5'-6" high, topped with logs. The water tower has a 10' high stone section topped by a 5' 6" section of logs with saddle-notched corners. Each section of the building has its own hip roof.

Lakefront Refectory (Lakeview Shelter), one of the many remaining New Deal structures at Gooseberry Falls State Park

Gooseberry Falls State Park

Gooseberry Falls State Park boasts one of the most extensive displays of work done by the CCC or any other New Deal agency in the state. Dozens of structures remain, including, the Concourse (Castle in the Park), the bridgehead refectory (Falls View Shelter), caretaker's cabin, water tower, a kitchen shelter (Lady Slipper Lodge), a refectory (Lakeview Shelter), two sets of stone stairs, a chain fence along the cliff at the picnic area, a pump house, stone picnic tables, fireplaces, drinking fountains, two latrines, a combination building (Campground Shelter), an ice house, and the Gitchi Gummi trail.

An Emergency Conservation Work Camp, SP-5 Company 1720, was established on May 3, 1934. SP-10 Company 2710, opened a tent camp on July 22, 1934. On October 5th, Company 1720 was transferred out of the park to Ely, Minnesota , and Company 2710 moved into their more permanent campsite west of the Upper Falls on October 20th during a heavy snowstorm.

Company 2710 consisted of 212 enrollees, mostly from Mankato, Minnesota. In their first year at Gooseberry, the men constructed one mile of road, four miles of foot trails and nineteen miles of fences.

The construction of buildings began in 1935, and the park became an official state park in 1937. The CCC camp remained open until July, 1941–the longest lifespan of any state park-based camp in Minnesota.

The lack of prior development, the dramatic setting, the long tenure of the CCC camp, and the skill of the camp members combined to make Gooseberry a showcase for what the New Deal agencies could accomplish.

The T-shaped kitchen shelter (now called the Lady Slipper Lodge) was the first building to be completed. The top of the T is a 50' x 28' enclosed shelter area that is now used for interpretive programs. This section was originally open to the

Kitchen Shelter (Lady Slipper Lodge), Gooseberry Falls State Park

weather. If the wind was off Lake Superior, however, such a structure provided little shelter, and the openings were filled in 1939.

The trunk of the T is a smaller kitchen shelter, separated from the main shelter by a large fireplace. The 9' opening on the west of this section is still open, but the side openings have been closed. The kitchen shelter took 3,228 man-days to build at a cost of $2,050.

The lakefront refectory (now the Lakeview Shelter) sits on a small hill overlooking the mouth of the Gooseberry River. This building included a concession area, a storage room, restrooms, and a partially enclosed shelter. Parts of the walls are entirely of stone, but some of the building is made of logs with saddle-notched corners. This building was completed in 1936 and also cost $2,050.

The bridgehead refectory (Falls View Shelter) was completed in July, 1939 at a cost of $4,390 and took 5,300 man-days. It evolved from a souvenir, pie, coffee, ice cream, and hamburger shop into a nature store/interpretive center. In 1995 it was closed, as work began on the new bridge and visi-

tor center. Once funds are available, this building will be restored and open to the public.

The 300' long concourse (affectionately called the "Castle in the Park") was built in stages from 1936 to 1940. The final section of the concourse to be built was the long stairway that leads to the base of the wall, where at one time there were restrooms.

The concourse was designed to look like a castle. The wall is 12' wide at the base, and in places, it extends underground to rest on solid rock. It is 20' to 25' tall. It now supports the Gateway Plaza, which offers panoramic views of the river valley.

Architectural concept sketch of the Concourse (Castle in the Park), Gooseberry Falls State Park

Some of the men who worked on the concourse liked to stand at highway level, fishing pole in hand and fishing line over the edge of the concourse, waiting for unsuspecting motorists to stop and ask if the fish were biting. One peek over the edge at the dry path below revealed the prank.

The water tower was built in 1936. The tower was built because efforts to locate a well in the picnic area failed. The 10,000-gallon tank was encased in the stone tower both to keep the water cool and to hide the tank. The tower rises 25 feet and is 17 feet across. When the

Benches on the Ledge. Construction of benches, picnic tables and outdoor fireplaces, Gooseberry Falls State Park

tank was first installed, 10,000 gallons would supply the entire park for a week. Today, that amount would not supply the campground and picnic area for one day in the summer. The tower is no longer used.

Thirty picnic tables (along with a number of outdoor fireplaces) were built in 1935. Three tables are near the Lady Slip-

per Lodge, seven are along the Gooseberry River near the mouth, and twenty were placed at the picnic area on Lake Superior. The tables have stone side supports with split-log seats and tabletops. Exposed to weather coming off Lake Superior, the wood deteriorated quickly, and the original logs were replaced long ago.

Combination Building (Campground Shelter) with CCC boy, 1994. Gooseberry Falls State Park

"Here lies a state park that will live in the years to come as a tribute to the nation's CCC and a monument to Company 2710, it officers and its boys."

—1941 newspaper epitaph

WEST CENTRAL PARKS

Charles A. Lindbergh State Park

Charles A. Lindbergh State Park was established in 1931. The park is named in memory of Charles A. Lindbergh, Senior, congressman from central Minnesota. His son, who became famous for his solo, trans-Atlantic flight, ran the family farm (the land that eventually became the state park) from 1918 to 1920.

When structures were being considered for the park, the Lindbergh family requested that development be limited. WPA workers built a picnic shelter, water tower, latrine, drinking fountains, and a retaining wall.

The picnic shelter was built in 1938. It is made of logs and features saddle-notched corners. The main entrance has a porch supported by log posts. Inside is a large stone fireplace. The kitchen still contains four cast iron cook stoves and the original sink. Windows and doors were not added to the building until 1939. The design for this building is the same as the shelter at Lake Bemidji State Park. The shelter and nearby water tower add a historic feel to the shady grove of the picnic area.

Picnic shelter at Charles A. Lindbergh State Park

Water tower in the picnic area, Charles A. Lindbergh State Park

Lake Carlos State Park Bath House

Lake Carlos State Park

Lake Carlos State Park was established in 1938 to provide recreational opportunities for the public in the midst of a premier resort area. Remaining WPA structures include a mess hall, crafts building, water tower, sanitation building, and bath house. The group center mess hall, built in 1941, and the nearby crafts building both have beautiful split stone fireplaces.

Veterans Conservation Corps begins development at Sibley State Park

Sibley State Park

A game reserve, established in 1917, Sibley became a state park in 1919. It is named for Minnesota's first governor, Henry Sibley, who loved to spend time in this area. Kandiyohi County operated Sibley Park until 1935. In that year, VCC Camp SP-7, Company 1785, "The Three Bear Camp," began the extensive construction that remains today.

Area residents were expecting a typical CCC camp of young men, but instead got a group of 200 experienced veterans. The New London Times reported (May 2, 1935): "We understand the camp will eventually have about 200 men—all veterans. Veterans who served 18 years ago will now serve us in a more pleasant way. We wish them joy. Planting trees in Sibley Park will be a lot more pleasant than planting white crosses in France."

All the buildings were made of pink and gray granite from Cold Spring and Rockville, Minnesota. The stone was so hard and difficult to split that the crews were able to use only a quarter of the stone supplied. When they finished their work at Sibley, they moved to Itasca State Park, where they worked on Forest Inn and other buildings.

The first projects at Sibley were at the Cedar Hill picnic ground, where they built a shelter, water tower, and latrine. Road construction also began early in the camp's history. The work ended up costing $750,000 and took three years to complete. In addition to the construction, the camp cleared 1,200 feet of beach and planted over 10,000 trees.

When the work was completed, it was the most extensive public recreational facility in central Minnesota. Sibley provides an excellent example of a well-planned park of that era, with functional recreation spots and well-designed traffic circulation.

The remaining structures, which are relatively unchanged from the New Deal era, include a shelter pavilion, pump

Construction gets underway at the Cedar Hill picnic ground, Sibley State Park

house, latrine, drinking fountains, a bath house, a fish cleaning house, an ice and wood house, the campground shelter, a combination building, a water tower, and, in the service area, a custodian's cabin, and garage and office.

At the Cedar Hill picnic area, the latrine building set the standard for the buildings at Sibley. Burt Morton, the LEM who led the project, was insistent about the quality of the white oak and granite that made their way into the building. He rejected many of the logs and stones that were delivered to the site.

The water tower in the Lakeview Campground rises 30 feet in granite and oak. Metal beams in the top of the structure once held a 5,000-gallon water tank, but the tower is no longer in use.

There is an interpretive exhibit near the beach that provides a glimpse of what life was like in the VCC camp.

Combination building in the Lakeview Campground, Sibley State Park

Lac qui Parle State Park

Though Lac qui Parle State Park was officially established in 1941, development work by the WPA had begun in 1938. The work in the park was just a part of a much larger effort—the Lac qui Parle Flood Control Project. Lac qui Parle Lake is a thirteen-mile long widening of the Minnesota River. The total project involved diverting the Chippewa and Lac qui Parle Rivers and establishing reservoirs for water conservation and flood control at Marsh Lake and Lac qui Parle. Smaller aspects of the project included the Watson Wayside, Lac qui Parle Control Dam, the Lac qui Parle Parkway, and the reconstruction of the Chippewa Lac qui Parle Mission.

WPA camps built three structures at Lac qui Parle State Park: the sanitation building, a kitchen shelter, and the model shelter.

The model shelter is one of the most unusual structures in the state park system and it is possibly the only WPA building of its kind in the nation. It houses a concrete relief map of the Minnesota River Valley and the Lac qui Parle Flood Control Project. The model is 50' long and 2'8" high. It sits on sand atop a concrete footing. This exhibit was part of an important promotional effort to gain public acceptance of the relief programs and their projects.

Concrete relief map and map model shelter at Lac qui Parle State Park

EAST CENTRAL PARKS

Interstate State Park

Interstate is located along a rocky gorge that rises from the banks of the St. Croix River. Established in 1895, Interstate is the second oldest state park in Minnesota to still operate as a state park. Prior to park designation and continuing today, Interstate is a world-renowned travel destination, receiving as many visitors as a large national park.

The New Deal structures remaining are located in two separate parts of the park. The Glacial Gardens area includes men and women's restrooms, a refectory, a drinking fountain, and stone walls. The campground/picnic area includes a sanitation building, a shelter/refectory, drinking fountains, and a combination building.

The development carried out in the 1930s treated this area as an outdoor geologic museum, where visitors could view and appreciate the unique rock formations. Camping and picnicking were not emphasized. The two areas of the park were kept separate to minimize overcrowding and to help traffic flow.

The structures feature basalt rock quarried within the boundaries of the park, most likely from a site where, in 1931, Highway 8 cut through.

The retaining wall near the river in the Glacial Gardens is 150' long and 8' to 10' high. The WPA crew that finished it in 1938 may have built upon an existing wall. Note also the well-planned placement of the buildings within the rocks of the surrounding landscape.

The Refectory at Interstate State Park's Glacial Gardens. Note how the rock construction blends with the surrounding landscape.

In the picnic area, the shelter/refectory is a T-shaped structure built with basalt and covered with a gable roof. The shelter has entrances in both the east and west facades. Inside the shelter is a large stone fireplace. A concession operated in the refectory until 1976, when that section was converted into restrooms.

The Combination Building was built from a design used first at Whitewater State Park. The use of construction materials unique to each park resulted in very different-looking buildings, even though the design was the same.

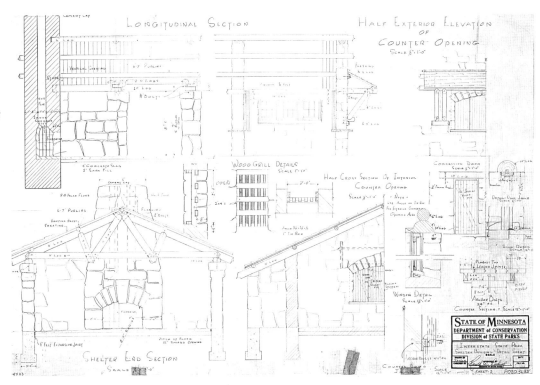

Original blueprint for the shelter/ refectory in the picnic area at Interstate State Park

St. Croix State Park

With more than 150 surviving WPA and CCC structures, St. Croix State Park contains Minnesota's largest collection of remaining New Deal era work relief program projects. St. Croix was also Minnesota's only National Recreational Demonstration Area (RDA), one of only 46 in the country, and the nation's second largest (slightly smaller than Custer State Park in the Black Hills of South Dakota). For this distinction, the park is designated a National Historic Landmark.

The RDA program was considered by many to be the most successful of the New Deal work programs. Paying farmers for their submarginal lands, creating recreational opportunities for the public and providing work relief through the WPA and CCC projects required multi-agency cooperation and embod-

Directional sign for the St. Croix Recreational Demonstration Area

ied the goals of all the program agencies.

There were five areas of concentrated development at St. Croix: park headquarters, Riverview Campground, and three group camps: St. John's Landing, Norway Point, and Head of the Rapids. These areas are spread out, several miles apart. The stone used in the structures is local sandstone, and much of the wood used was harvested within the park.

You will need a map (available at park headquarters) and plenty of time to see the New Deal legacy at St. Croix. The group centers and service areas are often reserved or

Headline from the St. Croix CCC newspaper. Many camps had their own newsletter, which served as an important communication and public relations tool.

The fireplace from Camp Yellowbanks still stands

have restricted access. Please inquire at the park headquarters for information.

Perhaps the place to start your visit is the site of one of the former CCC camps (Yellowbanks, SP-6). Here you'll find a trail with interpretive signs that describe the camp life and accomplishments of the CCC in the St. Croix RDA. You can see foundations, roadways, and the fieldstone fireplace of the camp's recreation hall. It's a fine, quiet spot to get the feel of what a CCC camp was like.

The Norway Point Group Center was built on a decentralized plan that was an innovation of the National Park Service. The camp was constructed in 1937 by the WPA, and opened in 1938 as a boys' camp. There are 45 structures here that date from the New Deal, including all of the cabins, the two large, central buildings, and even the drinking fountains.

In the Riverview Campground area, take a look at the St. Croix Lodge, which now contains the park's interpretive center, a shelter, and restrooms. The lodge was built between 1937and 1938. It is constructed of local sandstone and logs. The central, shelter area features a large sandstone fireplace, a log truss ceiling, and furniture built by the CCC. The interpretive center section of the lodge has been expanded twice.

Craft class at the Norway Point Group Center

From the interpretive center, follow the campground road through the Riverview Loop. On the outer loop of these roads, the water tower, pump house, combination building, and two cabins date from the New Deal. Peek through the windows of the old pump house on the outside of the loop (the pump is still inside) and admire the craftsmanship of this little building.

There are 46 remaining structures at the St. John's Landing Group Camp. The plan for this camp follows the same decentralized pattern as Norway Point. Except for the garage and shop building, which were built by the VCC, the WPA constructed this camp. It opened on August 3, 1936, and it served 9 to 14 year-old girls from the Twin Cities.

St. Croix Lodge in the Riverview Campground area

Stop at the fire observation tower (built in 1936 by the WPA) and the Kettle River overlook (built by the VCC).

The Head of the Rapids Group Center contains 19 New Deal structures, including the office/ infirmary, latrines, mess hall, craft building, and 11 of the cabins.

The Head of the Rapids camp was designed mainly for handicapped children for whom a more centralized plan, with shorter distances between buildings, was more appropriate.

Other New Deal era structures within the park include the entrance portals, several remote adirondack-style trail shelters, and many miles of roads and trails. The park entrance road was built on an existing railroad bed, but gentle curves were added and the road was landscaped to

Arts and crafts program at St. John's Landing Group Camp

make the drive more pleasant. The improvement of this road and the construction of the campground road were among the first projects undertaken at St. Croix. Another 25 miles of secondary road were added throughout the New Deal era.

Entrance portals. Original lettering has been changed from "St. Croix Area" to "St. Croix State Park."

MINNESOTA RIVER VALLEY PARKS

Minneopa State Park

The land for Minneopa State Park was purchased in 1905 to help preserve Minneopa Falls and to provide recreation for residents of nearby Mankato.

Minneopa has seven New Deal era structures, including a kitchen and concession building, latrine, pump house, drinking fountain, custodian's cabin, and a garage/office.

The kitchen and concession building was constructed by the WPA in 1939. The largest section of this T-shaped building contains the concession and kitchen area. The trunk of the T is a storage area. The walls are made of sandstone, with some wood siding on the gables and the storage area. The kitchen area now contains interpretive exhibits.

Also built in 1939 by the WPA, the latrine is a beautiful example of wood and stone construction. It is made of sandstone that extends 4" below ground. Bell-shaped stone screens topped with finely detailed gable roofs screen the entries. Box beams run above the windows on the east and west, and 6" x 6" beams project out from beneath the gable roof.

WPA-constructed steps in the Falls Area, Minneopa State Park

The latrine in the Falls Area, Minneopa State Park

Flandrau State Park

The New Deal era structures at Flandrau State Park are among the most distinctive in the state park system. In keeping with the effort to use local styles and materials, the principal buildings were designed to reflect the German heritage of the surrounding New Ulm community. The roofs have steep pitches, and the walls, made of quartzite, are built with small stones, set in non-linear patterns, to give these buildings an "Old World" feel.

The concept of Flandrau State Park was intimately tied to the philosophies of the New Deal. There were few lakes in this part of the state, and the State Executive Council purchased 805 acres in 1934, in hopes of building a dam and reservoir. This project would provide flood control, recreation for the region, and work for the unemployed. First named Cottonwood River State Park, the name was changed in 1945 to honor Charles E. Flandrau, a local lawyer and Indian agent during the 1860s.

Campground kitchen shelter, Flandrau State Park

Flandrau was originally named Cottonwood River State Park

The central development in the park was the construction of a concrete dam across the Cottonwood River. Floods and subsequent removal of the dam have eliminated any remains. CCC Camp S-14 constructed the dam and the kitchen shelter. This camp consisted mostly of veterans for the first year, but after that its population was young men, like most CCC camps.

WPA Transient Camp WC-12 was established separately from the CCC camp, overlooking "Lake Cottonwood." The WPA camp buildings were intended to eventually serve as a group camp for the "underprivileged" but their most immediate use was for housing German prisoners of war during World War II.

All other remaining period buildings at Flandrau were built by a "regular" WPA camp.

The New Deal era structures are clustered in three spots within the park.

The main use area of the park includes the beach house, entrance portals, a drinking fountain, and a kitchen shelter. The beach house, built in 1938, is a large, T-shaped building divided into three sections: the center section was a concession area; a shelter area was in the west section; and the beach house with restrooms and changing rooms was in the east section. The entry, located in the center of the building, leads to a passageway through to a terrace flanked by a stone wall. The shelter section of the building features a beamed ceiling with enormous trusses. Three timber light fixtures are mounted in the ceiling. At one end is a stone fireplace. This building may be one of the first in the state park system to be designed for winter use.

The service area behind the park office, built by the WPA, includes the superintendent's residence, a garage and work-

Completion of the dam across the Cottonwood River

shop, and a stone retaining wall. The residence, like the beach house, is built of quartzite. The house also has the same steep-pitched roof as the other buildings. Access to the service area may be restricted. Check at the park office.

The site of the WPA transient camp is now the park's group camp center. It includes eight barracks, latrines, the old WPA office, a stone bridge, and earthen berms on both sides of

The beach house at Flandrau State Park may be the most unique building in the state park system.

the river (the remains of the dam). This site can only be reached from another entrance to the park. Sometimes the gate is locked or the center occupied by groups. If you wish to visit this site, contact the park office.

The WPA camp at Flandrau State Park once housed German prisoners of war during World War II and is now the park's group camp.

Fort Ridgely State Park

Fort Ridgely State Park was established in 1911 as a memorial to the old fort built in 1853. The fort held troops until about 1867. After that, it was left to deteriorate. Homesteaders, who used it to build their homes, took much of the original fort building material.

By the 1930s, the fort had all but disappeared. In 1934, CCC Camp SP-12 was sent to develop recreational facilities and begin restoration of fort buildings. However, in 1935, when the state's allotment of CCC camps was lowered, Camp SP-12 was closed. In 1936, the Minnesota Historical Society, with the

Unpainted barracks await CCC enrollees to move in from their tent camp at Ft. Ridgely State Park.

Water tower/garage building at Ft. Ridgely State Park

help of a new VCC camp, which had been moved here from Camden State Park, began an archaeological excavation of the old fort site. The project uncovered and identified the foundations of eight buildings, which make up an outdoor interpretive site today.

The park's New Deal era structures include a combination building, drinking fountain, picnic tables, a fireplace, two latrines, a shelter building, the restored commissary building, the fort foundation restorations, and a water tower/garage.

The water tower/garage building, located just up the road from the fort, includes an office, pump room, and workshop.

The building is made of Morton gneiss. The stonework of the tower goes up 21 feet; above that level it is made of wood, and it is capped with a conical roof. The rest of the building is topped with a gabled roof that slopes down to a height of six feet.

The CCC camp once staged a work strike. They refused to work outside in sub-zero temperatures unless they were given better clothing and a shorter workday. Perhaps this, or related incidents, had something to do with why this camp was closed.

PARKS OF THE SOUTHWEST

Camden State Park

Camden State Park was established in 1935 but VCC Camp SP-11 (Company #2713) had already begun work by August 10, 1934. Because their planned work at Camden was finished in September of 1936, the men of SP-11 were transferred to Fort Ridgely after the CCC camp there had been closed.

The WPA carried out several projects after the VCC left. They dismantled the VCC camp buildings (three of these buildings were rebuilt at the park's group camp) and they built the swimming instructor's cabin and the ice and wood house.

The remaining New Deal structures include the bath house, swimming instructor's cabin, a recreational dam and lake, drinking fountains, a shelter and concession building, a sanitation building, the custodian's cabin, a warehouse and garage, and an ice and wood house.

Two drinking fountains, constructed by the VCC, stand in the picnic area. These fountains are the only ones in the state made of uncut fieldstones. They rest on a bed of flagstone; the fieldstones were piled on that, and the fountains were topped with a large, naturally flat stone.

Most of the rock used to construct the bath house at Camden was cut from this local boulder.

Camden State Park Bathing Pool on a Sunday afternoon, 1939

CAMDEN STATE PARK
BATHING POOL

Bath house at Camden State Park, 2002

Lake Shetek State Park

Lake Shetek was chosen as the site for a new park in order to relieve some of the pressure on nearby Camden State Park.

The WPA camp buildings were unusual in that they were intended as permanent structures—many such buildings around the state were designed to be temporary, even though some of them are still in use! The Lake Shetek camp structures were built as a group camp for the "underprivileged" once the work of the WPA was done. Eventually, however, this area of the park was sold. Since that time the buildings have been used as a private church camp.

The plan for Lake Shetek State Park was one of the most extensive of the New Deal Era. The original plan called for a series of causeways, connecting five islands thereby providing a road that would cross the lake. Five of the causeways were built, but the one connecting to the mainland was never completed. The remaining structures include a bath house, drinking fountains, kitchen shelter, sanitation building, a mess hall, and the crafts and recreation building.

The bath house, constructed between 1939 and 1940, is built on a high bank next to the shore of Lake Shetek. The cen-

Loon Island causeway on Lake Shetek

tral section of the building originally contained rest rooms, a concession area, and storage. This section features loggias, or passageways, along the sides.

The bath house sits on stone retaining walls. A large ter-race overlooks the lake. The dramatic 6 foot-wide staircases run around the sides of the terrace and then down to the shore. The terrace and stairs make this one of the most attrac-tive designs in the park system.

The bath house at Lake Shetek State Park, then and now

Blue Mounds State Park

Blue Mounds State Park was established in 1937. The WPA carried out the main construction in the park.

The remaining structures in the park, which include the latrine building and two dams, are exquisite examples of the design philosophy of the New Deal era. All are built of native Sioux quartzite.

The upper dam was built in 1938 and blends nicely with the surrounding quartzite bed of Mound Creek. The dam was a cooperative project between the WPA, the Emergency Relief Administration, and the Minnesota Department of Conservation, Division of Drainage & Waters.

The dam at Blue Mounds State Park showing an outcrop of Sioux quartzite

SOUTHEASTERN PARKS

Whitewater State Park

Whitewater State Park was established in 1919. CCC Camp SP-4 opened on April 28, 1934, and a second CCC camp, SP-9 moved in on July 1, 1934. Camp SP-4 (Company 1723) moved out of the park on September 30th of that year, and SP-9 (Com-

The original Whitewater State Park entrance sign

pany 2709) was left to carry out the extensive work plan. In October, 1935, SP-9 was also closed, even though development was not complete.

In February, 1936, a WPA transient camp opened in the park. This camp used the same site as the CCC camps (south of the Whitewater River and east of State Highway 74). The camp housed transients (unemployed men who were wandering, looking for work) but it also employed local residents. The camp buildings were used dur-

Vehicle bridge at Whitewater State Park

ing World War II to house German prisoners of war who worked on local farms. Later it served as a youth camp until it was destroyed by a tornado in 1953.

Whitewater holds one of the most diverse and interesting collections of structures in the state. The stonework is native limestone, giving Whitewater a different feel from other parks. The plan for the park is also noteworthy since it had to deal with Highway 74 running right through the park.

Remaining New Deal structures include entrance signs, picnic shelter, dam and swimming area, beach building, footbridges, kitchen shelter, drinking fountains, picnic

WHITEWATER STATE PARK
BATHING **POOL**

Swimming area and beach building, Whitewater State Park

tables, retaining walls, restrooms, combination building, custodian's cabin (former manager's residence), warehouse, garages, pump house, water supply tanks, and a stone loading ramp for the quarry.

The rectangular picnic shelter is made with native limestone. There are 16' openings in the ends and 25' openings in the long sides of the building. These long openings are divided into three parts by 12" square posts. Limestone pillars are found in each corner of the shelter. The gable roof is supported by six large trusses. Note that the gable ends are open, so the truss work is exposed. The shelter, built by the CCC, remains one of the most beautiful in the state.

The WPA built several footbridges over the Whitewater River. One in particular is noteworthy. It stands about 12' above the river. The bridge was built with enormous 12" x 18" beams, 30 feet long. There is a one-foot rise in the bridge from each end to the center, which gives it an elegant, arched look. There are limestone

Limestone picnic shelter at Whitewater State Park

retaining walls on both sides, with steps on the west and a landing on the east. It is the only surviving bridge of its type in the state park system.

PARKS WITH LIMITED NUMBERS OF REMAINING NEW DEAL STRUCTURES

Temperance River State Park
Temperance River State Park did not become a state park until 1957, well after the New Deal era. However, the stonework along Highway 61 was built by CCC Camp F-19, a forestry camp based at Tofte, just down the shore. The stonework along the highway parking area was built of black gabbro, and the stone steps and walls along the Cauldron Trail were built of fine-grained diabase.

Cascade River State Park
Cascade River State Park didn't become a state park until 1957. However, a CCC camp was located within the future park boundaries and many of the trails and much of the landscaping along Highway 61 was done by the CCC. The "highway beautification" work done by this camp, which included a concourse along Lake Superior and the opening of Spruce Creek Wayside may have been the first such project anywhere in the country. The stonework along the river trail was made of two unusual types of rock that were taken from highway cuts west of the town of Hovland: monzodiorite (dark red) and ferrodiorite (black).

Judge C. R. Magney State Park
During the late 1930s, the park was the site of a transient work camp established by the State of Minnesota. The camp, named after the director of the division of forestry at that time, Grover Conzet, was located in the area of the present-day campground. Some remains of camp structures from that time still exist. Contact the park office for details.

Monson Lake State Park

Workers from the VCC camp at nearby Sibley State Park developed Monson Lake State Park. The road construction was a WPA project. Monson Lake became a state park in 1937, and it is notable for being virtually unchanged since that time. The two buildings constructed by the VCC camp still remain: a combination building and a sanitation building.

Split Rock Creek State Park

Split Rock Creek State Park was established in 1937. The dam (partially built of Sioux quartzite), the stone arch highway bridge, and the water tower were built by the WPA, which also planted 5,000 trees in the area.

Beaver Creek Valley State Park

Acquisition of the land for Beaver Creek Valley State Park began in 1936 and, in 1938, a small (up to ten men) WPA crew began work there. The only work completed by this crew was the entrance road, the picnic grounds, and a few trails.

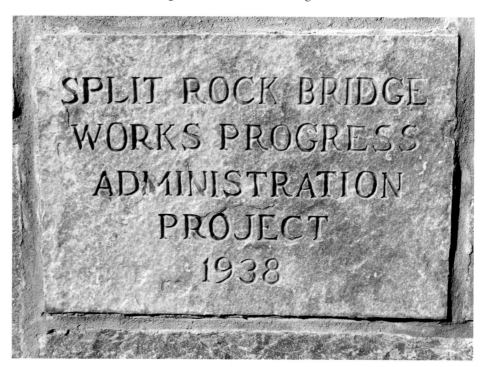

Plaque from the stone arch highway bridge at Split Rock Creek State Park. Dedication plaques can still be found on many period structures throughout the United States.

> There are many more structures to be found in state parks dating from this era than we had room to include. This is just a sample. There are also hundreds of other structures dating from the New Deal to be seen throughout Minnesota. Please visit the Minnesota Historical Society website for more information.
>
> We hope that this field guide to remaining New Deal era structures has piqued your interest in this important part of our country's history. Keep your eyes open for other evidence of the New Deal wherever you may travel.

Fire observation tower at St. Croix State Park built in 1936 by the WPA

GLOSSARY

abutments   the parts of a bridge or dam that anchor the structure to the shore

basalt   a hard, dark gray or black, volcanic rock

berm   an earthen ridge or embankment

CCC   the Civilian Conservation Corps, a work relief program of the New Deal

corbel (also corbelled)   a bracket of brick, stone, or wood that juts out to support construction elements above

dike   a low wall of earth or rock built to hold back floods

ECW   Emergency Conservation Work (the original, legislative name of the CCC)

fieldstone   stones gathered rather than quarried

gabbro   coarse-grained, dark, volcanic rock

gable   where a wall extends up to form a triangle beneath a roof's angled surfaces

granite   coarse-grained rock with visible crystals and noticeable shine

hip (hipped) roof   where two angled surfaces of roofs meet

latrine   restroom or sanitation building

loggia   covered, open-sided walkway

Basalt used in the construction at Interstate State Park

Corbelled log work supporting log roof beam at the lodge, St. Croix State Park

One of the gabbro types used in the construction at Jay Cooke State Park

Hipped roof on the water tower/latrine building at Oldenburg Point, Jay Cooke State Park

Sioux quartzite used in the construction of some of the structures at Flandrau, Blue Mounds, and Split Rock Creek State Parks

mantel   the frame or shelf above a fireplace

masonry   construction utilizing stone or brick

non-linear   in a random pattern or in a pattern that doesn't follow straight lines

quartzite   a hard rock resulting from the recrystallization of quartz sandstone

refectory   snack bar or concession area

rough-hewn   logs not smoothed to a finished surface

saddle-notched logs   logs whose ends have been notched to fit together with other logs like a saddle on a horse

spillway   a structure built to control, but not stop, water flow

sill   window ledge

transient work camp   a camp set up to provide work and housing for the homeless

truss (trusses)   the supporting timber(s) in the ceiling structure of a building

VCC   Veterans Conservation Corps, a work relief program for veterans of World War I

WPA   Works Projects Administration or Works Progress Administration (two names for the same agency)

Detail showing saddle-notched logs at Oldenburg Point, Jay Cooke State Park

One of the log truss systems used at Gooseberry Falls State Park

BIBLIOGRAPHY

Here is a list of references and resources that we found useful and interesting during the production of this book:

Anderson, Rolf. Final Report: Minnesota CCC/WPA Rustic Style Historic Resources, 1988.

Banks, Ann, ed. *First-Person America*, Knopf, NY, 1980.

Barber, Edward W. Interview by Ben Thoma and Gladwin Lynne, June 8, 1994.

Cohen, Stan, *The Tree Army: A Pictorial History of the Civilian Conservation Corps, 1933-1942*, Pictorial Histories Publishing, Missoula, MT, 1980.

Davis, Kenneth S., *FDR: The New Deal Years, 1933-1937*, Random House, NY, 1986.

Degler, Carl N. ed, *The New Deal*, Quadrangle Books, Chicago, 1970.

Dudley, William, ed. *The Great Depression: Opposing Viewpoints*, Greenhaven Press, San Diego, CA, 1994.

Freidel, Frank, *Franklin D. Roosevelt: Launching the New Deal*, Little, Brown, 1973.

Good, Albert H., *Park and Recreation Structures*, Princeton Architectural Press, New York, 1938.

Gower, Calvin W., "The CCC Indian Division," *Minnesota History*, Spring, 1972, pp 3-13.

Heegard, Harley. Interview by Amy K. Rieger, July 12, 1993.

Hella, U.W. "Judge." Interview by Amy K. Rieger, August 10, 1993.

Johnson, Frederick, "The Civilian Conservation Corps: A New Deal for Youth," *Minnesota History*, Fall, 1983.

Johnson, Frederick, "The Civilian Conservation Corps: Public Works or Panacea?" *Public Works*, October, 1980.

Lacy, Leslie Alexander, *The Soil Soldiers: The Civilian Conservation Corps in the Great Depression*, Chilton, 1976.

Law, Reuben. Interview by Amy K. Reiger, Ben Thoma, and Ron Miles, June 23, 1993.

Leuchtenberg, William E., *Franklin D. Roosevelt and the New Deal*, Harper & Row, NY, 1963.

McElvaine, Robert S., *The Depression and New Deal: A History in Documents*, Oxford, NY, 2000.

McElvaine, Robert S., *The Great Depression: America, 1929-1941*, Random House, NY, 1993.

Miller, Perry H., *Roosevelt's Forest Army: A History of the Civilian Conservation Corps*, Montpelier, VT, 1981.

Nelson, Edward P. and Barbara Sommer, eds. *It Was A Good Deal: The Civilian Conservation Corps in Northeastern Minnesota*, St. Louis County Historical Society, 1987.

Nixon, Edgar B., *Franklin D. Roosevelt & Conservation, 1911-1945, vol. 2*, General Services Administration, National Archives and Records Service, Franklin D. Roosevelt Library, Hyde Park, New York, 1957.

Otis, Alison T. et al. *The Forest Service and the Civilian Conservation Corps: 1933-1942*, (FS - 395)USDA, 1986.

Ryan, J.C., *The CCC and Me*, J.C. Ryan, Duluth, MN, 1987.

Salmond, John A. *The Civilian Conservation Corps, 1933-1942*, Duke U., Chapel Hill, 1967.

Schubert, Edward. Interview by Amy K. Rieger, July 21, 1993.

Sperling, Harry. Interview by Amy K. Rieger, July 28, 1993.

Thoma, Ben. The Civilian Conservation Corps and Itasca State Park, 1984.

Thoma, Ben. Itasca State Park Civilian Conservation Corps Projects, 1936-1942, 1993.

Thoma, Ben. Itasca State Park Old Timer's Cabin, Minnesota DNR, 1994.

Tweton, D. Jerome, *Depression: Minnesota in the Thirties*, North Dakota Institute for Regional Studies, Fargo, 1981.

Wallin, Roy. Interview by Amy K. Rieger, August 18, 1993.

Watkins, T.H., *The Great Depression: America in the 1930s*, Little, Brown, Boston, 1993.

Zinn, Howard, *New Deal Thought*, Bobbs-Merrill, Indianapolis, 1966.

WEBSITES

United States National Archives and Records Administration
www.archives.gov/index.html

Franklin D. Roosevelt Presidential Library and Museum
www.fdrlibrary.marist.edu

New Deal Network
http://newdeal.feri.org/index.html

Minnesota Historical Society
www.mnhs.org/index.html

Iron Range Research Center
www.ironrangeresearchcenter.org/index.html

We encourage you to check out these resources to learn more about this fascinating period of state and national history.